MACRAMÉ

First published 2021 by
Guild of Master Craftsman Publications Ltd
Castle Place, 166 High Street, Lewes,
East Sussex, BN7 1XU, UK

ISBN 978 1 78494 640 1

PUBLISHER **Jonathan Grogan**
PRODUCTION MANAGER **Jim Bulley**
EDITOR **Sian Hamilton**
SUB-EDITOR **Christine Boggis**
DESIGNER **Claire Stevens**
ILLUSTRATOR **Sian Hamilton**

Set in TT Norms Pro
Colour origination by GMC Reprographics
Printed and bound in the UK

PICTURE CREDITS
All photography by Laurel Guilfoyle, Sian Hamilton and Tansy Wilson

CONTENTS

mandala macramé

Tansy Wilson

The meaning of the word mandala, loosely translated, is 'circle', and it is considered a spiritual and ritual eternal symbol – so using round embroidery rings as a frame for your designs is the perfect way to make these really gorgeous wall hangings. I have shown three easy styles primarily using the square knot. Just remember, the process of macramé in itself is quite meditative.

YOU WILL NEED
Beaded Mandala
- 3mm (⅛in) macramé cotton cord
- 10 x 5mm (³⁄₁₆in)-hole glass beads
- 20 x 4mm (⁵⁄₃₂in)-hole gold beads
- 20cm (8in) embroidery ring
- Scissors
- Comb

Simple Mandala
- 5mm (³⁄₁₆in) macramé cotton cord
- 15cm (6in) embroidery ring

Tasselled Wool Mandala
- 4 ply multicoloured wool
- 26cm (10½in) and 13cm (5in) embroidery rings
- 8 x 4mm (⁵⁄₃₂in)-hole pony beads

BEADED MANDALA

1 Using 3mm (⅛in) cord cut 80 x 65cm (25½in) lengths. You will only use eight lengths for each petal of the flower pattern, so tie your first eight lengths on to the embroidery ring using the lark's head knot (see page 94) for each one.

2 Move the very first and last pair of cords away from the now central six pairs, as these end cords are not yet needed. Tie a row of three square knots (see page 96) using all the cords of the central six pairs.

3 Take the two left cords hanging out of the bottom left of the left square knot and move to one side. Using the two cords directly next to this, tie a square knot with the two left cords coming out of the bottom of the middle square knot.

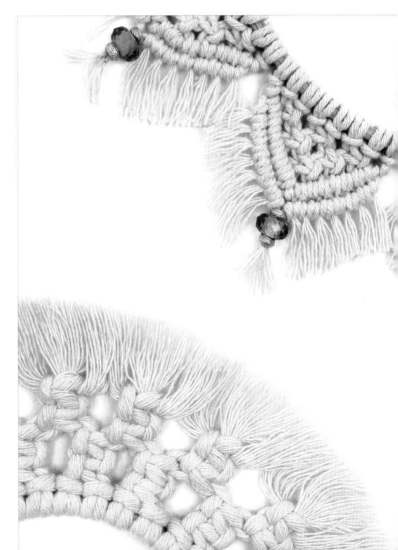

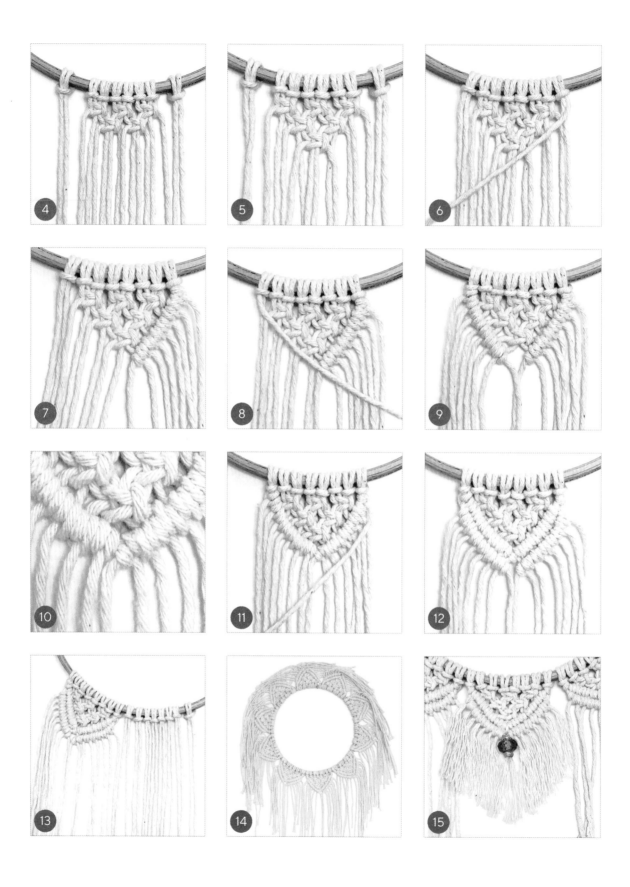

TOP TIP
Add a drop of super glue to the very ends of your cords. Once dry, this makes the cord really easy to thread through the hole of a bead.

4 Tie another square knot using the next cords along, which results in two square knots in a row under the three tied in step 2 and another pair of cords not being used at the very right.

5 Finally tie a square knot with the four central cords, which results in a triangular pattern of square knots, as in this image.

6 Now slide the first and last untouched pairs of cords, not used from step 2, back down to the rest of the cords and, starting on the right, use the far right-hand cord and pull it diagonally across the macramé triangle to use as your lead cord.

7 Take the cord hanging immediately to the left of this lead cord and tie a clove hitch knot (see page 99) around the lead cord. Take the next cord hanging to the left, which is now the one that comes out of the bottom of a square knot, and tie a clove hitch knot around the lead cord. Keep methodically tying clove hitch knots all along the lead cord until you come to the bottom square knot of the triangle. You will only tie clove hitch knots with the two cords hanging out from the bottom right of this knot.

8 Now take the far left-hand cord and use this as your lead cord.

9 Repeat step 7, tying clove hitch knots methodically this time from left to right all along the lead cord. Finally, tie clove hitch knots with the two cords coming out of the left-hand side of the bottom square knot.

10 To bring the two lines of knots together, take one as your lead cord and tie a final clove hitch knot around it with the other. This image shows I took the right-hand cord to be my lead and tied the knot with the left-hand cord. It can be either way!

11 You can leave the design here, but I decided to add another row of clove hitch knots, again starting on the far right with my lead cord.

12 Follow steps 7–9 to tie the double row of knots directly under each other, as in this image. You will see I have not joined the very bottom together yet as I will do this later on in this project.

13 Take your next eight cords, fold them in half and attach to the embroidery ring using the lark's head knot.

14 Repeat steps 2–13 to make another petal. Then repeat steps 2–13 a further eight times so you end up with ten petals evenly spaced around the entire circumference of the ring.

15 Remember where I hadn't tied the bottom row together in step 12? Well, this step adds a bit of sparkle to your design. Take beads with large holes like these pretty gold and glass beads, thread the bottom two cords that you would have tied through the holes and then tie. Combing and trimming the fringe into shape adds that perfect finish. Repeat this step for all your petals.

SIMPLE MANDALA

16 Cut 38 x 50cm (20in) lengths of 5mm (³⁄₁₆in) macramé cord. Take two pieces, fold each in half and attach to your embroidery ring using the lark's head knot (see page 94). Then tie two square knots immediately under each other using all four cords.

17 Take another two pieces from your cut cords, fold each in half and again attach to your embroidery ring, using the lark's head knot, to the right-hand side of those already added, then tie two square knots (see page 96) immediately under each other using the four cords.

18 Missing out the first two cords from the left, make another two square knots on top of each other with the next four cords along. This will leave you with two cords on the right not used.

19 Take another two pieces from your cut cords, fold each in half and again attach to the right of everything on your embroidery ring, using the lark's head knot, and then tie two square knots immediately under each other using the four cords.

20 Take the two cords that were not used on the right in step 18 and make another two square knots with the two cords on the left of the square knots just added in step 19.

21 Keep adding two cords at a time, always working anticlockwise and following steps 19 and 20 until you have gone all the way around your ring. The last join will use the cords left out in step 18 to secure all the square knots together.

22 As you have used thick cord you can comb out the fringe and trim it to any desired shape. I've simply echoed the circle. Hairspray can help set the fringe if it's a bit floppy.

  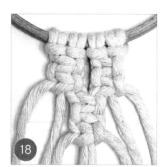 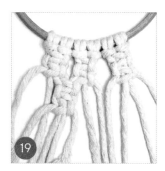

  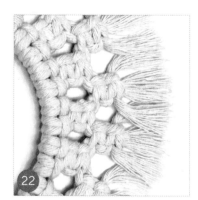

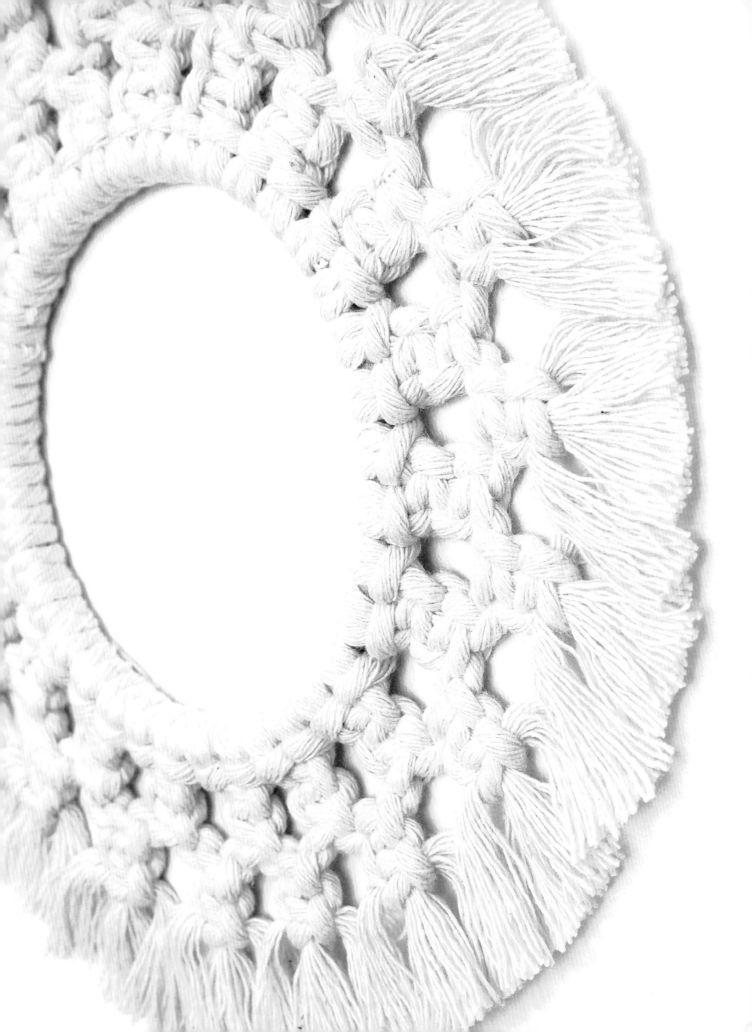

TASSELLED WOOL MANDALA

23 In this design I glued two embroidery rings together at one point only and used 4 ply wool. Cut 16 x 2.5m (8ft) lengths of wool, fold each piece in half and attach them all to the smaller ring using the lark's head knot (see page 94).

24 Take the first four strands and tie a square knot (see page 96). Tie the next four strands into a square knot and keep repeating, tying eight square knots in total using all the cords and following the underside of the small ring.

25 Miss the first two strands of wool out, then tie a square knot with the next four strands. Keep tying square knots all the way along, until you end up with two strands of wool not used on the right-hand side.

26 For the next row of square knots, start by using the two left-hand strands not used in step 25 and the next two along. This will again result in a row of eight square knots using all the wool strands.

27 Keep repeating steps 25–26 to make alternate rows of square knots until you get near to the bottom of the larger ring. Wool is very stretchy, so for an open-holed effect, don't get too near the bottom so you can pull the wool tight.

28 I worked left to right, so starting with the very left strand, take it behind the ring. Pull the end up around the front of the ring, then take it behind itself and back behind the ring, then feed the end through the loop created at the bottom of the ring and pull tight to secure in position.

29 Repeat step 28 so you tie each individual strand on to the bottom of the embroidery ring, controlling the tension of the wool to evenly space out the holes between the square knots.

30 For a final touch I added pony beads to each cluster of four strands, gluing them in place rather than tying a knot so the fringe stayed nice and straight.

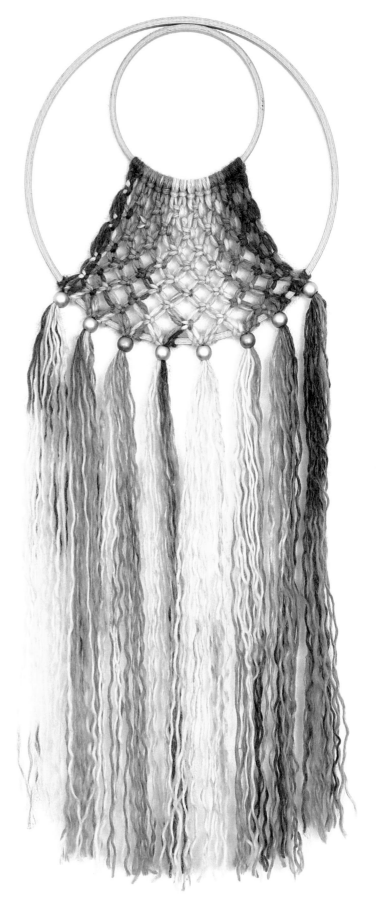

shelf chic

Tansy Wilson

Macramé is famous for being associated with plant hangers, and this project is based upon the same principle – but the shelves give it a modern twist. Once you have mastered macramé knots, the design combinations for this project are endless!

YOU WILL NEED
- 4mm (⁵⁄₃₂in) macramé cord
- 50mm (2in)-diameter curtain ring
- 120 x 15 x 2cm (4ft x 6in x ¾in) planed timber
- 10mm (⅜in) drill bit and hand or power drill
- Hand saw
- Sandpaper
- Scissors
- Comb

Optional
- Paint and paintbrush
- 12 x 18mm (²³⁄₃₂in) diameter wooden beads (or 18mm (²³⁄₃₂in) dowel)

1 Cut your three shelves to the desired size. Mine are 35 x 15 x 2cm (14 x 6 x ¾in), all cut from a 120cm (4ft) piece of planed timber. Sand the edges smooth using sandpaper and drill a 10mm (⅜in) hole in each corner of each piece. You can then paint each shelf or leave them natural!

2 Cut 8 x 6m (19¾ft) of 4mm (⁵⁄₃₂in) macramé cord and thread each piece half way through the curtain ring so you have 16 lengths of cord each 3m (10ft). If you've painted your shelves, a nice touch is to paint the curtain ring to match.

3 Try to arrange your cords so four of them sit on top of the other four. Then take a cord from the left back pair and a cord from the right back pair and begin to tie a square knot (see page 96). Pull gently, as you don't want the cords underneath to get too bunched up.

4 Complete the square knot, ensuring it sits snugly under the curtain ring, then make another two square knots directly underneath, going down all the cords.

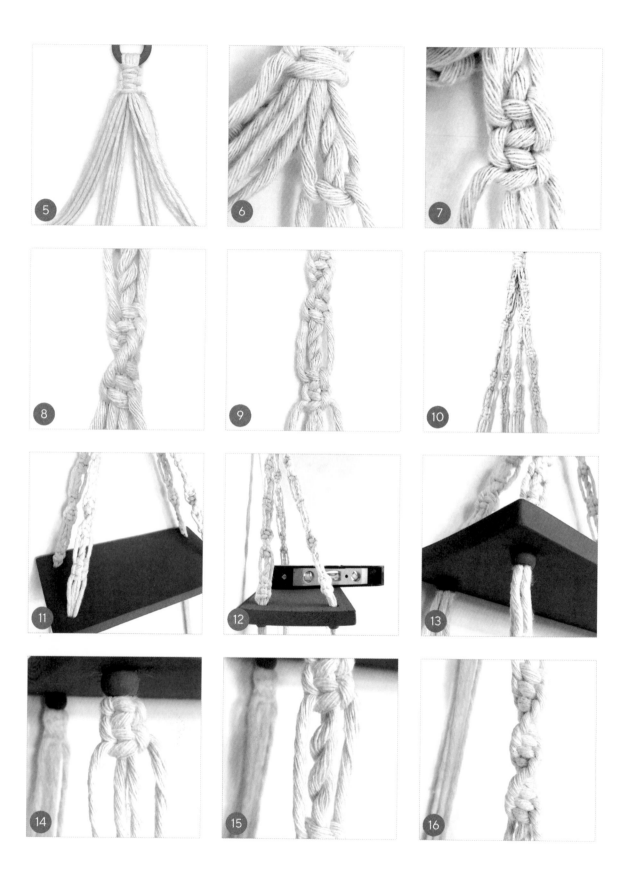

5 Separate the 16 cords into four groups of four and splay them out so you don't get in a muddle. Try to ensure the cords don't overlap each other too much, for a much neater look. It helps to hang the entire piece up to get the measurements and levels as best as possible.

6 Now you can start with your first group of four strands. Splay them out so they are not tangled, select the middle two and twist together a few times. While holding the twist, take the two outer cords and start to make a square knot about 4cm (1½in) down from the curtain ring.

7 Continue to finish the square knot and tie another one directly underneath.

8 Twist the centre two ropes a few times and start another square knot approximately 4cm (1½in) down from the underside of the last square knot. This time do not finish the square knot but repeat the same tying direction and the square knot will start to twist on itself. Keep tying this half square knot (see page 98) six times so you achieve a full twist.

9 Take the centre two cords coming out of the bottom of the twist, and again twist them together a few times and tie two square knots, approximately 4cm (1½in) down.

10 Repeat steps 6–9 methodically, working on each group of four cords. The trick is trying to get them as evenly matched as possible, but don't sweat too much as it can be adjusted a little once the shelf goes on.

11 Take your first shelf and feed the four back left cords through the back left hole, and then the four back right cords through the back right hole and so on until all the cords are through the holes of your shelf.

12 As your shelf will hang from a nail in the wall you will have the two front sets of cords longer than the back ones to make the shelf horizontal. Keep pulling the ropes from underneath the shelf until it is as level as possible.

13 Now you can tie a knot to secure the shelf in position. However, if you are good at DIY, you can drill a 10mm (⅜in)

hole into a large wooden bead. Alternatively you can drill the 10mm (⅜in) hole into the top of a piece of wooden dowel and then saw into 10mm (⅜in) lengths to obtain donut-shaped beads, which also give a great finish.

14 Whether you've tied a knot or used a wooden bead, you now go back to working with one set of four cords and tie two square knots on top of each other.

15 Twist the two middle cords together a few times, then start to form a square knot approximately 4cm (1½in) down.

16 As in step 8, do not finish the square knot off but again keep tying it in the same direction so it spirals around and down. Repeat this 12 times to get a lovely spiral.

TOP TIP

Using a little spirit level is the easiest way to know your have a perfect horizontal for each shelf.

17 Twist the centre two cords around themselves a few times and tie two square knots approximately 4cm (1½in) down.

18 Take your second shelf and push each set of four cords through the corresponding holes in the shelf. Again adjust the height where necessary and tie or use wooden donut beads to secure the shelf in position.

19 Repeat steps 14–18 to make the last decorative supports and to add the final shelf.

20 Tie a further two square knots on top of each other directly underneath your knots or beads, then cut any excess cords with scissors. I went for a nice long tassel that I combed out to balance the design.

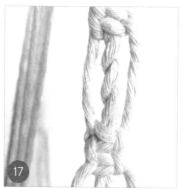

geometric mirror

Sian Hamilton

This mirror is stunning hung on a wall, but it takes patience and time to create. Don't rush this design, as you want the knotting to be precise. This pattern is complex and assumes you have some knowledge of macramé already.

YOU WILL NEED

- Metal rings, 2 x 35cm (14in) and 1 x 50cm (20in)
- 2mm (¹⁄₁₆in) macramé cord in two contrasting colours (I used Welcome Yarn by Barbante in Grey and Light Grey)
- 50cm (20in) round mirror (I used a mirror tile)
- Super glue
- Scissors

1 You'll need three rings for this design. They need to be metal to hold the weight of the mirror and the tension placed on them by the macramé. The overall size of this mirror is 50cm (20in): one ring needs to be the same size as the mirror and two rings need to be smaller as the inner rings. One goes on the front and the other on the back.

2 This design takes a lot of cords! Cut 9 x 1m (3ft) lengths in both colours. Group them into 12 strands. Then fold each one in half and attach them to the 35cm (14in) ring with lark's head knots (see page 94), alternating the colours. You should end up with eight sections of 12 strands doubled up to create 24 cords per section.

3 Start with a dark grey colour section. Push the light grey cords on each side away from your working area to give you more room. Make a row of six square knots (see page 96). This should use all the cords in this dark grey section.

4 Skip the two outer cords and make another row of square knots so they sit between the knots above.

5 Repeat the square knot rows, skipping two more cords each time to make a triangle.

6 Go around the ring, creating identical triangles with all the colour sections.

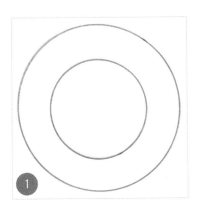

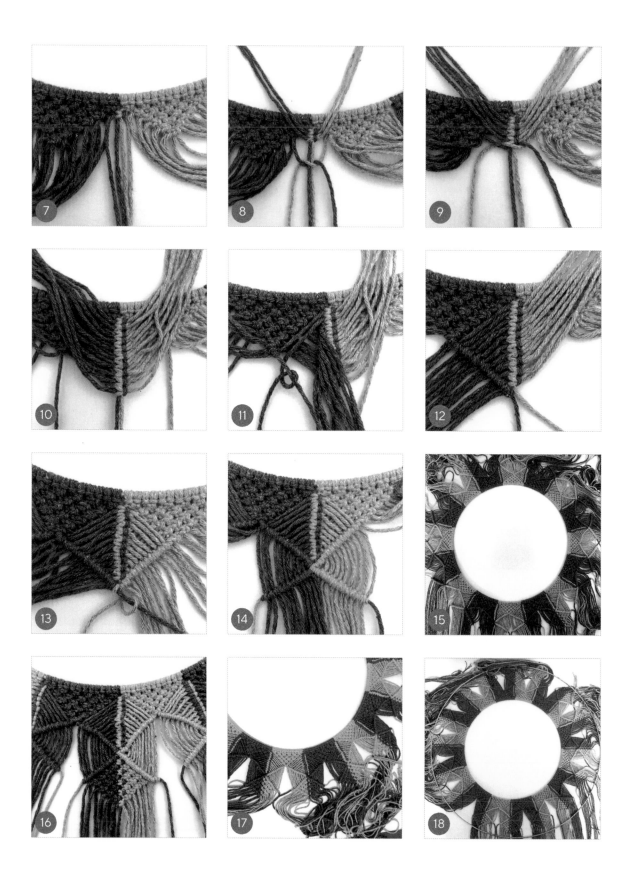

7 Place the ring with two triangles facing you (dark grey on the left and light grey on the right), pick up the outer cords for each colour that are sitting side by side (up by the metal ring). These will be the anchor cords (cords you tie the knot around) for a column of square knots. Pick the next cord along on each side and tie the first square knot. You'll see this knot is a mix of both colours.

8 To make the column, pick up the next cord down on each side (these are called the knotting cords) and create a square knot. Be careful to only pull the cords as tight as they need to be to keep the knotting flat.

9 If you pull the cords too tight the column will start to bunch up. Gently release the knotting cords if this happens until it all lays flat. As you move down, place the knotting cords from the square knot above away from you so you can clearly see what you are doing.

10 Use all the cords from the edges of the triangles. Don't use the anchor cords from the final square knot at the bottom of the triangle. When you have used all the available cords you will have ten square knots. If you have 11, release the final one as you have gone too far.

11 The next step is to make a line of clove hitches (see page 99) using the knotting cords from the column made in step 10. Pick up the right-side anchor cord from the bottom square knot on the dark grey triangle on the left.

Pull all the dark grey cords from the left side of the column over to the right so you can see what you are doing. There are so many cords in this design that you want to keep your working area clear, as that makes it easier to grab the correct cord.

Pick up the dark grey cord from the first square knot on the column and make a clove hitch.

12 Repeat with each of the dark grey cords on the left side of the column. Try to keep the clove hitch line as straight as possible. Finish the line with the left side anchor cord on the column (this should be dark grey). You should have used all the colour-coordinated cords. Refer to the step photo to check your work is correct.

13 Repeat steps 11–12 for the other side of the column, using the light grey cords. Remember to work slowly and steadily to make sure you are using all the cords in the correct order. When you reach the end of the hitch line, pick up the dark

grey core cord and tie the final hitch knot with the light grey core cord from the right side line (as shown in the step photo).

14 Continue using the same core cords to make more clove hitches. Follow the step photo for reference.

You want to create a cross shape and use all the same cords as the lines above. It can be tricky to get the hitch lines to stay straight if you pull the knots too tight, so watch out for that and try to keep the lines as straight as you can.

This design section should use all the cords, starting with the right-side anchor cord on the dark grey (left) triangle (cord coming out of the bottom square knot) to the light grey left-side anchor cord on the light grey triangle. If done correctly, you will have a dark grey core cord on the right side and a light grey core cord on the left side with the opposite colour used for the hitch knots.

15 Repeat steps 7–14 to create the same design between each triangle section.

16 Make a square knot diamond in the bottom of the cross shapes. Start with the four cords at the top of the bottom cross section. The two left cords should be dark grey and two right cords light grey. Make a square knot.

On the next row, there should be a dark grey knot on the left and a light grey knot on the right. This creates a brick pattern of knots.

Each diamond should have nine rows, each row increasing in knots up to five and then decreasing back to a single knot.

17 Repeat step 16 on all sections.

18 Place the 50cm (20in) metal ring over the macramé and check that your design will fit inside the ring. If it doesn't, you will need to do a little tweaking to stretch or contract it.

TOP TIP

If you are making a different size, make sure you have enough of a frame to hold the mirror in place.

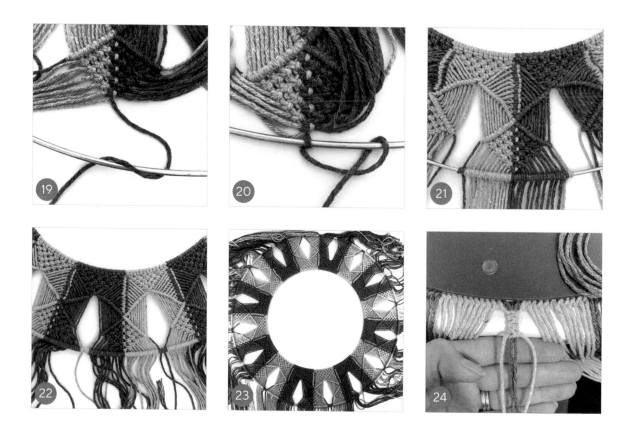

19 The macramé design is attached to the larger ring with clove hitch knots, using the metal ring as the core cord. For each section, start in the middle using the anchor cords from the bottom square knot. Tie the two anchor cords first, then work outwards.

Pick up a dark grey cord from the bottom of a square knot and start the hitch knot by wrapping the cord around the ring. Come underneath the ring, over and under again towards the left. This first knot is tricky as you are just wrapping and not knotting!

20 Pull the cord until the square knot is sitting just above the ring. Wrap the cord around the ring again on the right side of the first knot. The cord should be sitting just under the ring already. From beneath the ring go over the ring and under, bringing the cord towards the left through the loop created. Repeat this for all the right-side dark grey cords and one light grey cord at the end.

21 Come back to the centre and make another hitch knot using the light grey anchor cord. Reverse the direction for all hitch knots on the left side. Wrap under the ring,

over and through the loop created towards the right. Pull tight and repeat until you have used all the light grey cords and one dark grey cord.

22 Repeat on all the sections. I worked on opposite sides to begin with to make sure the inner 35cm (14in) ring was sitting centrally.

23 After you have knotted the whole design to the larger ring, check it looks central.

24 To secure the macramé onto the mirror a second 35cm (14in) ring is used. To start, turn the macramé front side down and place the mirror also front side down over it. Find a section where there are two dark grey cords with light grey cords either side. Use the dark grey as anchor cords and make a row of four square knots. Turn the macramé and mirror 180 degrees and make another set of four square knots, using dark grey as anchor cords and light grey as knotting cords.

25 Place the 35cm (14in) metal ring in the centre of mirror. Use a measuring tape to make sure that there is a 15cm (6in) space between the ring and mirror edge all the way around.

Bring the two dark grey anchor cords you were just using under the ring, over the top and make three or four square knots using the same cords to hold the ring in place. Turn the macramé and mirror again.

Repeat on the opposite side to secure the 35cm (14in) ring in place. At this point be precise and spend time making sure these first two knotted lines are even. You need to work on both sides so the ring will not slide around as you connect the rest of the cords.

26 Bring the light grey up to the inner ring. Take them under the ring and down either side of the square knots already there.

27 Make a few square knots with these cords to secure them.

28 Go around the edge securing cords in the same way using steps 24–27. There should be eight sections with two dark grey cords sitting between two light grey cords and eight sections of two light grey cords sitting between dark grey. Work evenly around the edge, as this will help keep the inner ring in place. You should have 16 sets in total.

29 These 16 pieces should hold the inner ring and mirror in place. Try holding the mirror upright to check it doesn't slide around, but is securely held in place. If you are happy, place a tiny drop of super glue on each of the cord ends. Be very careful of super glue on mirror backs as it can cause ghosting, so work carefully or place a piece of paper between the mirror and the cords you are gluing.

As the mirror is heavy and will hang on a wall the glue will make sure that none of the knots come undone.

30 Using all the loose cords that are sitting between the tied sections, make hitch knots using the inner ring as the core cord, as you did to secure the macramé to the 50cm (20in) ring in steps 19–20.

31 This will make the edge of the mirror neat and tidy.

32 Keep going until every cord is tied on to the inner ring.

33 Add a little glue to the edge of the inner ring, making sure not to glue the ring to the mirror. Use a piece of paper if needed. This is just to keep the cords from coming undone.

34 When the glue is dry trim off all the loose ends. The inner ring works as the hanging hook for the mirror, so you will not need any other type of hook.

cool cushion

Sian Hamilton

Decorative throw cushions make a room look cosy and stylish. Instead of purchasing off-the-shelf varieties, why not make your own? This project uses a standard coloured cushion. You can use either a cushion cover or a simple colour-coordinated cushion as the base for this design.

YOU WILL NEED

- 4mm (⁵⁄₃₂in) macramé cord (I used 100m (328ft) single twist Welcome Yarn by Barbante in Dark Grey)
- Working board and 6 fold-back clips
- Measuring tape
- 40cm (16in) cushion in a coordinating colour
- Needle and colour-coordinating thread
- Pins
- Scissors
- Masking tape and extra clips (optional)
- Crochet hook (optional)

1 Follow the steps on page 102 to set up a working board. For a 40cm (16in) cushion cut 56 x 1.5m (5ft) lengths of cord.

For this design each cord will be tied individually to the line using a clove hitch (see page 99). Pick up a cord and place it under the line with the end sitting above the line at about 10cm (4in). Bring the long end from below the line, wrap it over in front of the line and back down behind the line on the left side. Refer to the step photo.

2 To complete the clove hitch, take the long end over the line again on the right side and bring the end through the loop created from the back. Refer to the step photo.

3 Pull the knot tight using both hands to hold the ends.

4 Repeat steps 1 and 2 to add all 56 cords.

5 Split the cords into two groups of 28. These cords are very long so they might get tangled up.

6 In the middle, where you have just split the cords into two groups of 28, pick up a a cord from each side and cross them over.

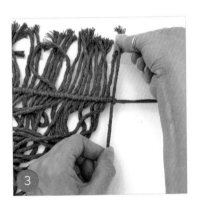

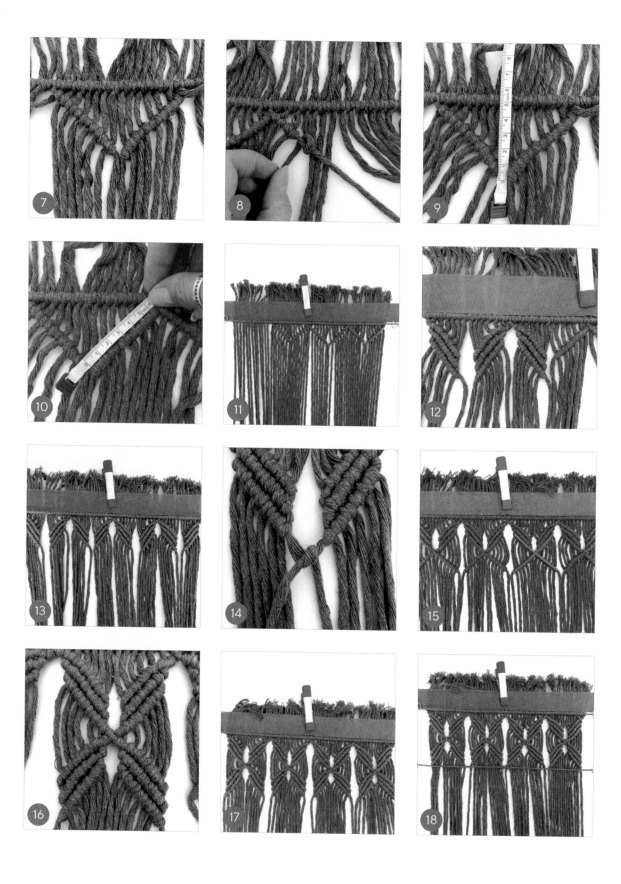

7 The first row is going to be a set of four downward-facing triangles. Each line uses seven cords, one cord as the core and six as knotting cords. The step photo shows one complete triangle. The next steps will walk through making this shape. You want to spend time getting this first triangle shape right, as everything else will follow the angle set with these first diagonal lines.

8 Make a line of clove hitch knots using the cord you crossed over in step 6 as the core cord. Hold the core cord at a 45-degree angle. Make knots with six strands. This can be tricky, so take your time. You want the cord above the knot to be straight and not too loose or too tight. Don't bunch the hitch knots up too much because the cords above the diagonal line will not be straight.

9 Ideally you need the depth of the triangle to be around 5cm (2in). At this early stage use a measuring tape to make sure you are setting the right depths. If you don't get this first bit right you'll have problems later.

10 The diagonal lines should measure around 5.5cm (2¼in).

11 The weight of all the cords can pull the centre of the macramé down, so I used masking tape to hold it in a straight line and an extra clip to keep it in place. This is optional but may help when you are knotting.

TOP TIP
Don't waste the cut-off ends of cords as they make fabulous tassels to use in any project – follow the steps on page 101.

12 When you have all of the first lines done on the triangles, add two more lines of hitches on each diagonal section.

13 The triangle sections should have three lines of clove hitches on each side. Start each line using the first cord on the outer edge as the core cord.

14 At the point of the triangles you want to connect the cords. Take the right-side core cord from the bottom line of knots and add another clove hitch using the core cord from the left side as the knotting cord.

15 Continue with this core cord and start knotting with the cords hanging below the triangle. The aim here is to turn each triangle shape into a cross (shown in red on the photo). Keep the hitch knot lines as straight as possible.

16 Add two more lines of clove hitches under the crosses.

17 Repeat step 16 for all four crosses.

18 At the centre of this design is a straight section that uses extra cords as the core cords. Cut a length of cord that fits across your board and clip it straight across under the crosses, so it is sitting touching the bottom diagonal lines.

19 Start the hitches using the cords in the centre, as that will help hold the core cord in place.

20 Go back to the left edge and knot every cord on to this core. Try to keep the design spaced evenly. Having the centre cords knotted already (step 19) will help.

21 If you struggle to pull the cord through when creating the clove hitches you can use a crochet hook to help.

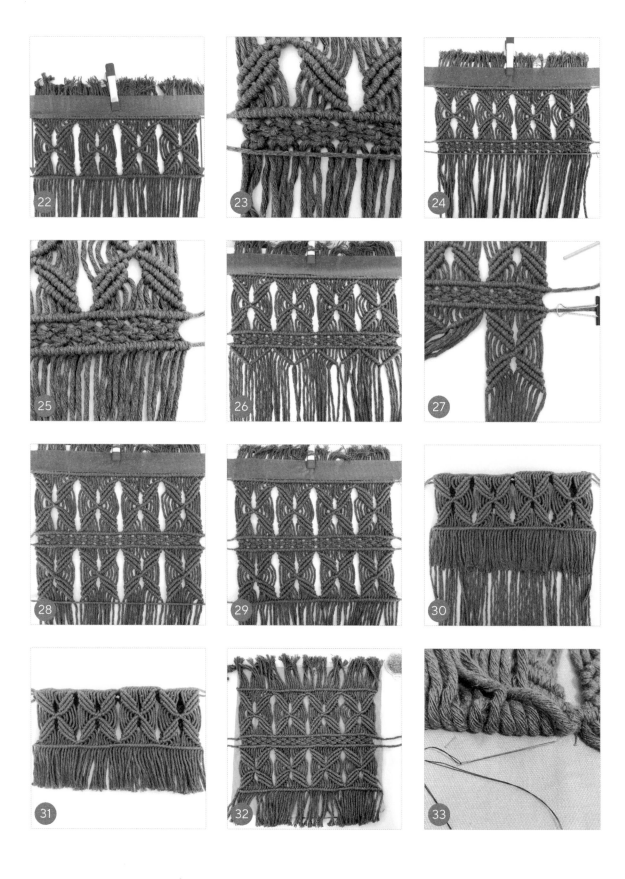

22 When you have completed the row, make sure the edges line up with the top. You want them to be the same width. If they are not, then tweak the knots to add width or reduce it.

23 Add three rows of square knots (see page 96) using all of the cords. The first and third rows start with the edge cords. On the second row, skip the first two cords to create the brick pattern.

24 Clip another cord line under the square knots, as you did in step 18.

25 Repeat steps 19–22 to create a second line of hitch knots under the square knots.

26 The design now repeats the top cross section. Follow steps 8–10 to make another set of diagonal hitch lines, but don't cross the centre cords over.

27 Repeat steps 12–17 to create four more cross shapes. Keep your measuring tape handy and keep measuring sections to make sure they are the same length as the crosses above.

28 When you have all four crosses finished, cut another length of cord and clip to the board under the crosses. You can unclip the lines holding the square knot section and use those clips to attach this line.

29 Repeat steps 19–20 to create the bottom edge hitch knot line.

30 Take the macramé off the board and fold in half at the square knot rows so that you can see the top (fringe) edge sitting over the cord ends.

31 Trim the cord ends to match the top edge, to create a matching fringe. Trim the top and bottom core cords

(the ones on the sides of the fringe) to match, but leave the side centre core cords long.

32 Flatten the macramé out and place it over the cushion. Centralise it and pin to the cushion to hold it in place.

33 Starting with one of the fringe ends, fold the fringe over the macramé and sew through the macramé and cushion with a needle and thread. Sew all the way around the cushion, making sure you catch cords and cushion fabric with each stitch.

34 Comb out the fringe using a nylon bristle styling hairbrush if you have one, or use your fingers to just separate the cords.

35 With sharp scissors, trim the fringe to sit level with the cushion edge.

36 On the sides with the long centre core cords, you can either make tassels with your scrap cord from step 31 (see page 101) and tie them to the sides, or just make neat bows with the cords and trim off any excess.

angel wings wall hanging

Tansy Wilson

Angel wings symbolise love, spirituality and protection, so what a fantastic subject for this beautiful wall hanging. Only the lark's head knot (see page 94) and the clove hitch knot (see page 99) are used, so despite its size, this is an ideal project for any beginner.

YOU WILL NEED

- 4mm (⁵⁄₃₂in) macramé cord
- Approximately 80cm (31½in) length of driftwood, dowel or garden stick
- Scissors

1 Cut 1 x 3.5m (11½ft) length of 4mm (⁵⁄₃₂in) macramé cord and attach it to the centre of your piece of driftwood using a lark's head knot. You could also use a wooden dowel or a stick.

2 Take the right-hand length of cord coming out of the lark's head knot and drape it to form a small loop, taking the cord end in front, over the top and then behind the driftwood, and then passing the end through the loop from the back to the front.

3 Take the same end and now move it to the right, going across the front of the loop, pass the end behind the driftwood, then up and over it, creating a smaller loop.

4 Now take the same end, pass it through this smaller loop going from front to back and pull the end down. This in effect has created a lark's head knot on the right-hand side of your driftwood.

5 Repeat steps 2–4 using the left-hand cord coming out of the central lark's head knot tied in step 1 to make another lark's head knot to the left-hand side of your driftwood.

6 Now cut 28 x 3m (10ft) lengths of your 4mm (⁵⁄₃₂in) macramé cord and, folding each piece, in half attach 14 of them using the lark's head knot to the left-hand loop, and the remaining 14 to the right-hand loop. You can tweak and tighten the loops at this step so all the 28 pairs of cords sit neatly together and look symmetrical.

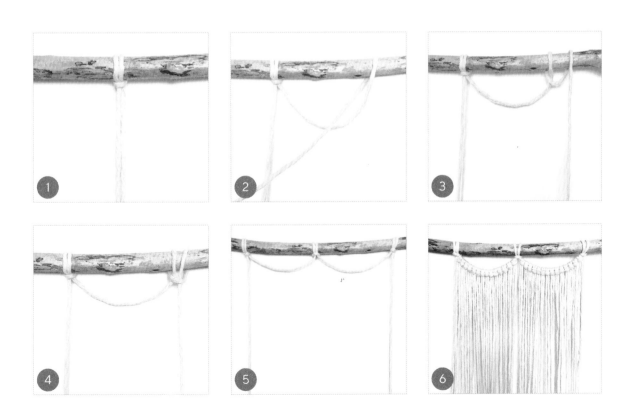

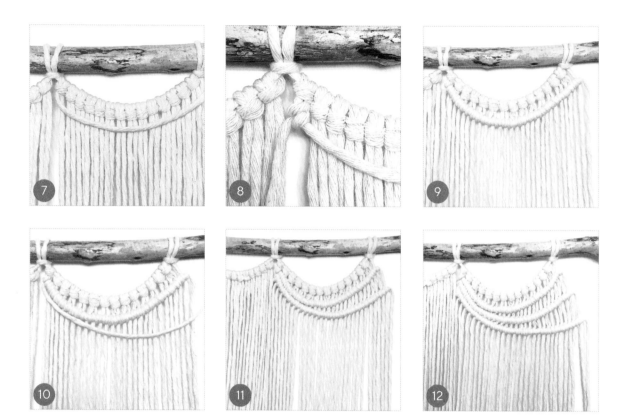

7 I started on the right-hand wing first so the following steps all apply to the right-hand side.

You are now only going to use the clove hitch knot. Take your leading cord, which is the first left-hand cord of the 28 cords hanging down from the right-hand side. Pull it to the right in a loose loop echoing the top loop.

8 Take cord number 2, hanging immediately next to the lead cord. It is the 'partner' cord from the original lark's head knot. Use a clove hitch knot to tie this cord on to the lead cord.

9 Working methodically from left to right, take the next cord, number 3, and tie it on to the lead cord using a clove hitch knot. Take cord number 4 and tie a clove hitch knot on to the lead cord. Keep repeating until you have tied all of the hanging cords on to the lead cord.

10 Go back to the centre of the piece and take another leading cord. Again, this is the very first left-hand cord hanging down from the right-hand group of cords.

11 Again work methodically from left to right, tying clove hitch knots all along the lead cord.

12 Repeat steps 10–11, always returning to the centre of the piece each time you complete a loop, to take a new lead cord and tie clove hitch knots on to it.

13 As you work your way down to the fourth row of clove hitch knots you can start changing the shape of the lead cord to create the wing shape. Continue this with the fifth and sixth rows.

14 Keep repeating steps 10–11 until you have added a total of seven rows of clove hitch knots to create a wing shape.

15 Go back to the centre, take the left-hand cord as the lead cord and make a clove hitch knot with the next partner cord along (cord number 2). Now pull the remainder of this partner cord and the lead cord across to the right, creating two lead cords.

16 Take cord number 3 along and create a clove hitch knot around both the lead cord and the initial partner cord, number 2. Take the remainder of cord number 3 and pull it to the right to create three lead cords.

17 Take cord number 4, tie a clove hitch knot around all three lead cords and add the remainder of this cord to

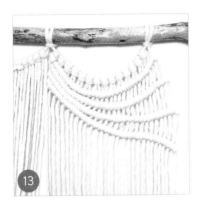

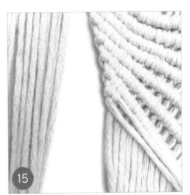

create four lead cords. Repeat, taking cord 5 and tying a clove hitch knot around all four lead cords, then add the remainder of this cord to create five lead cords. Finally take cord 6 and tie a clove hitch knot around all five lead cords. You will see how the clove hitch knots get fatter each time.

18 You can at this point roughly trim the bottom of just the right-hand cords and, if they are long enough, use these offcuts for the following steps. If they are not long enough you need to cut 16 x 60cm (24in) lengths to create a fringe for the right-hand wing. Fold one 60cm (24in) length in half and tie on to the right-hand pair of cords between the bottom two rows, using a lark's head knot.

TOP TIP

When tying a large project it is best to hang it up so the cords hang straight and don't get buckled. To create a hanger, attach a cord at either end of your driftwood using a lark's head knot and simply tie the four ends together at the centre top.

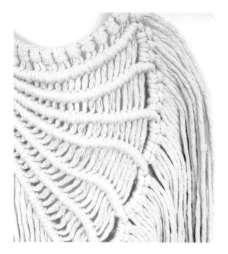
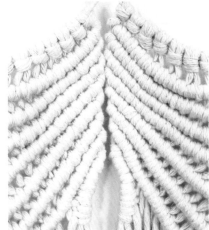

19 Fold another 60cm (24in) cord in half and tie it to the same pair of cords between the bottom two rows. Keep repeating until you have filled in this section.

20 Repeat steps 18–19 to tie a fringe all along the right-hand side of your wing. You may need more than 16 cords, just depending on how big the spaces are between your rows.

21 You now need to repeat the entire macramé process, steps 7–20, to create the left-hand wing – but this time your

lead cord working from the centre will be the far right-hand cord on the left side. Try to keep the shapes of each row as symmetrical as possible for a more realistic wing effect.

22 Once you have tied and completed both wings you can start trimming the overall shape using sharp scissors. I have created a gentle 'V' shape, leaving the fringe quite long, but at this step you can design your own wing shapes.

deckchair decor

Tansy Wilson

If like me you have a mouldy deckchair in the garden shed, don't throw it away but revamp it instead. Removing the tatty material and using this project to guide you through making a macramé seat creates this stylish and comfy chair!

YOU WILL NEED
- 9mm (⅜in) cotton rope
- Scissors
- Sticky tape
- 3 x 10mm (⅜in) beads with 4mm (⁵⁄₃₂in) hole
- Deckchair frame

1 Whether you already own a deckchair or need to buy one second hand, make a note of how the cover sits on the frame. Check the chair is stable and decide if you want to paint the frame a funky colour or rub it back with sandpaper if it needs a clean. Finally cut away the existing fabric. Fold the deckchair back up so the aperture where the fabric was is facing you, ready to start your macramé.

2 The following measurements are based on a standard adult-sized chair with the removed fabric measuring approximately 110cm (43⁵⁄₁₆in) long x 45cm (18in) wide. Using 9mm (⅜in) cotton rope, cut 24 x 7.5m (25ft) lengths. Wrap a piece of sticky tape around each cut to prevent the rope from fraying.

3 Fold your first 7.5m (25ft) length in half and, using a lark's head knot (see page 94), attach it to the top bar of the deckchair where the fabric was. It is important that the loop of the lark's head knot faces the back of the frame. This stops the knot from slipping when you sit in the chair. Repeat this step to attach all 24 lengths of rope to the frame.

4 Working from the left-hand side, take the first four ropes and make a square knot (see page 96). Repeat, working across all the ropes. You will end up with 12 square knots.

TOP TIP
If you are buying cotton rope it often comes in 15m (49ft) bails. This means there may be slight colour differences with different batch numbers. If this is the case, factor it into the design.

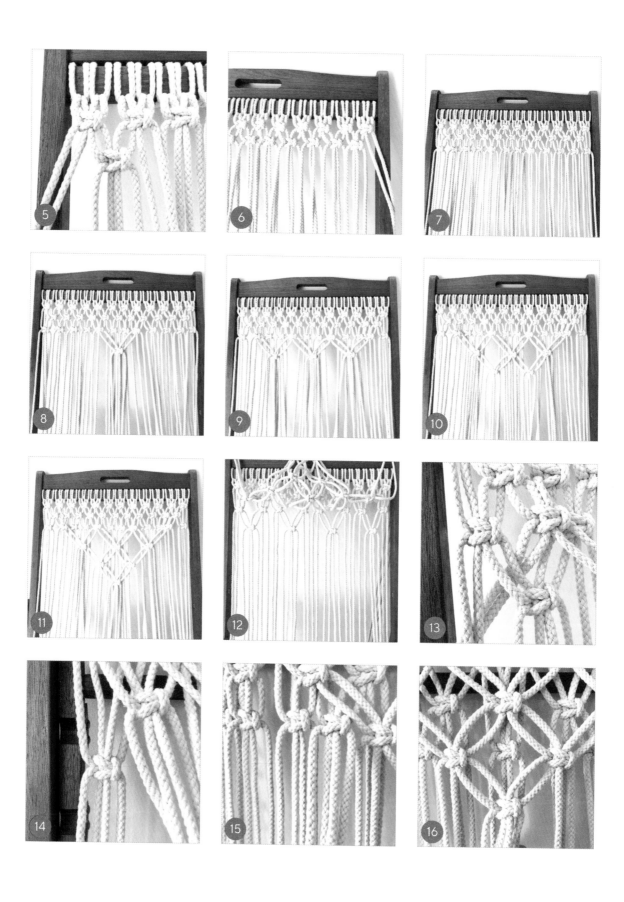

5 Starting from the left-hand side again, take the first two ropes hanging down and pull to one side. Then make another square knot with the next four ropes.

6 Continue to make square knots until you get to the right-hand side where the final two ropes will also be left untied. This creates a row of 11 square knots.

7 Repeat step 4 to create a third row of 12 square knots using all 24 ropes.

8 Counting in from the left-hand side of the third row, take the two right-hand ropes coming out of the bottom of the fifth square knot along. Counting in from the right-hand side, take the two left-hand ropes coming out of the bottom of the fifth square knot along. Tie these four into a square knot.

9 Counting in from the left-hand side of the third row, take the two right-hand ropes coming out of the bottom of the second square knot along and form a square knot with the two left-hand ropes coming out of the fifth square knot along. Counting in from the right-hand side on the same row, take the two left-hand ropes coming out of the bottom of the second square knot along and form a square knot with the two right-hand ropes coming out of the fifth square knot along to form the 'V' pattern, as in this image.

10 Working with just the three new square knots at the bottom of each 'V', take the two right-hand ropes of the first left-hand square knot and create another square knot with the two left-hand ropes coming out of the middle square knot. Take the two right-hand ropes coming out of the middle square knot and make another square knot with the two left-hand ropes coming out of the right-hand square knot.

11 Make a final square knot using just the two right-hand ropes coming out of the bottom of the left knot and the two left-hand ropes coming out of the bottom of the right-hand knot to form this large triangle pattern.

12 Pick up this new top layer of square knots and place it out of the way, exposing the ropes underneath. Missing the first two left-hand ropes, create a square knot with the following four ropes. Miss four ropes and create another square knot. Repeat so you have four square knots in a line.

13 Bring the top layer moved out of the way in step 12 back down. The four square knots created in step 12 should be in line with the three square knots created in step 9.

Take the two left-hand ropes coming out of the bottom of the first left-hand square knot on the top layer created in row three, feed them behind and pull the left of the two right-hand ropes of the first left-hand square knot created in step 12.

Mirror this for the right-hand side. Take the two right-hand ropes coming out of the bottom of the last right-hand square, not on this top layer created in row three, feed them behind and pull the right of the two right-hand ropes of the first left-hand square knot created in step 12.

14 Make a square knot with the first four ropes on the under layer: the first two and the two you fed underneath in step 13.

15 Working just on the under layer on the row created in step 14, make square knots all the way along under the top layer. Move this top layer out of the way to see more easily.

16 As you work along the under layer row, your square knots should be aligned in the middle of the square knots tied in the top layer to create an even pattern.

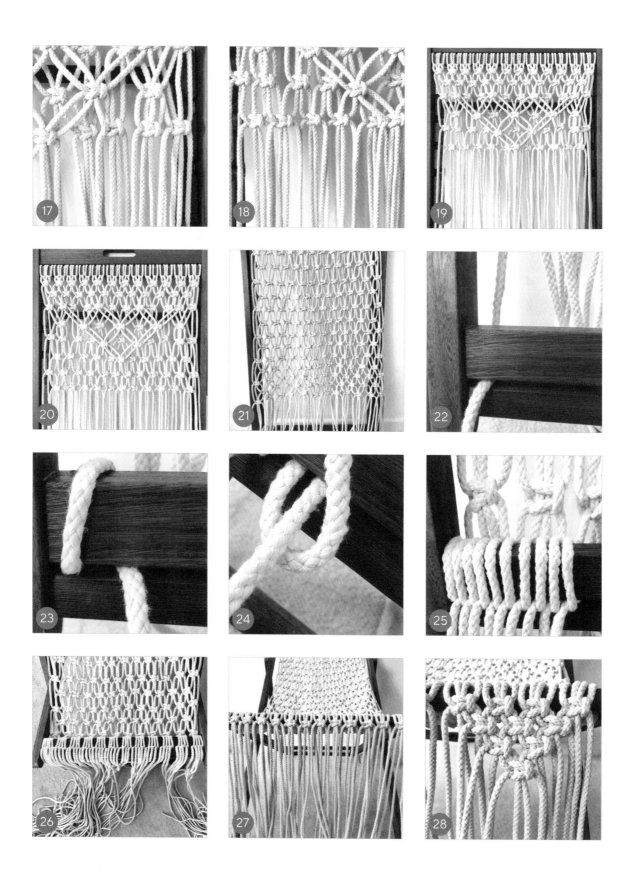

17 Continue methodically making square knots along this row with the ropes on the under layer until you come to the last four ropes on the right-hand side. Now use the two right-hand ropes fed behind in step 13 to make the last knot.

18 Starting at the left-hand side, take the first two ropes and pull to the side. Create a square knot with the next four ropes. Tie two more square knots along this row. For the fourth knot, use the two right-hand ropes from the under layer and the two left-hand ropes coming out of the bottom of the left square knot on the top layer created in step 10. It should be in line with the bottom square knot from the top layer.

19 Continue with this row and make another two square knots in the under layer. Then take the two right-hand ropes coming out of the right knot of the top layer tied in step 10 and the next two ropes along in the under layer to create the seventh square knot in this row. Continue this row with a further three square knots all in a line, leaving you with two right-hand ropes.

20 Working from the left-hand side, create another row of square knots all the way along to the right-hand side of the chair. When you get to knot 6, you will use the two left-hand ropes coming out of the bottom knot of the top layer. Knot 7 will use the two right-hand ropes coming out of the bottom knot of the top layer. Create another row of square knots working left to right, missing out the first two ropes.

21 At this step, all your ropes will have realigned and you will be back to tying on one layer. Continue making alternate rows of square knots until you get approximately 10cm (4in) from the bottom bar of the deckchair.

22 Push all your ropes behind the frame of the chair and, taking the very first left-hand rope, feed it from the back to the front of the bar you are going to tie it on to. This is going to be the same bar that the fabric was originally around.

23 Take this rope up in front of the bar, around the rope behind itself and back down behind, feeding back through the bar from back to the front.

24 Then take the end of this rope and feed it through the loop created around the bar, pulling really tightly so the last row of square knots pulls down to the bar.

25 Work methodically along each rope, repeating the pattern of feeding the end of the rope from the back of the frame to the front. Up in front of the bar and around and behind itself. Back down behind the bar coming through

again from back to front and finally feeding the end through the loop at the front and pulling as tightly as possible.

26 Once you have tied all of the ropes on to the bottom bar, open up the deckchair so you can see all the ropes spilling over the front edge. You can at this point determine the length of the fringe you want and cut the ropes using scissors.

27 The following steps are completely optional. Instead of just a cut fringe at step 26, you can tie a macramé pattern of your choice or follow this simple pattern to make a knotted fringe. Tie 12 square knots all along the bar edge.

28 Working with the first four square knots at one end, create a second, third and fourth row of square knots to form a triangle of knots, as in this image.

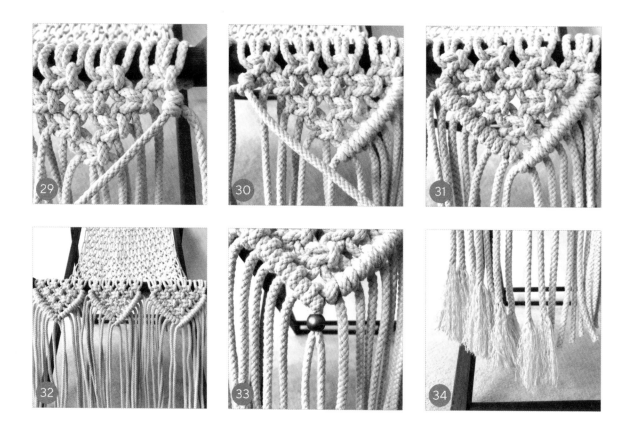

29 Take the end rope as your lead rope and create a clove hitch knot (see page 99) around it using the next rope in.

30 Keep making clove hitch knots along the lead rope until you come to the bottom centre square knot. Create another two clove hitch knots using the two right-hand ropes coming out of the bottom square knot. Take the left-hand rope and use as a lead rope.

31 Make clove hitch knots along this left lead rope all the way to the bottom, finishing with the two left-hand ropes coming out of the bottom square knot. Then make another clove hitch knot to join the two lines together.

32 Repeat steps 28–31 to make another two triangles of knots along the front of the chair hem.

33 Where the clove hitch knots join is an ideal spot to thread on a pretty, large-holed bead as an extra detail.

34 Finally you can cut the remaining ropes into point shapes using scissors and even use a comb to make the fringe fluffy.

lampshade

Sian Hamilton

Making a macramé lampshade can be tricky and is not for the complete beginner! If you are new to this craft, start with an easier project and build up to this one.

YOU WILL NEED
- Lampstand (minimum height 25cm (10in))
- 20cm (8in) utility ring lampshade frame
- 3mm (⅛in) macramé cord (I used 100m (328ft) 3 ply Bobbiny in Natural)
- 10cm (4in) shade carrier
- 192 x clear 8mm (⁵⁄₁₆in) pony beads with 5mm (³⁄₁₆in) holes
- Tape
- Scissors

1 You'll need a lampstand for your shade and a utility ring lampshade frame. I used a 20cm (8in) one as that matched the size of the lampstand well. If you have a bigger lampstand, get a utility ring to match.

2 Cut 64 x 1.5m (5ft) cords and tape the ends on each cord. This will stop them unravelling and help when you need to add on the beads.

3 Attach all the cords to the lampshade using lark's head knots (see page 94). Fold the cords in half, matching the ends so you end up with equal-length strands all the way around the utility ring. Most rings have three metal bars holding the central ring that attaches to the lampstand. To make sure you have your cords spaced as evenly as possible, attach 21 cords to two of the sections and 22 cords to the third section.

4 To start the design, make a row of square knots all the way around (see page 96). Make a second row of knots using two cords from the left knot and two cords from the right knot on the first line. This makes a brick pattern.

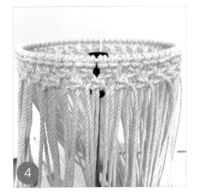

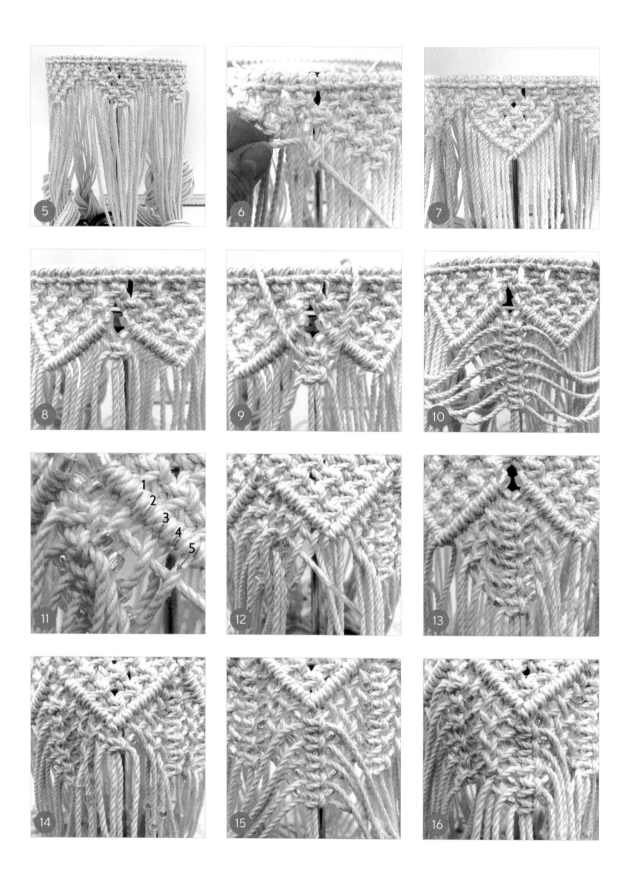

TOP TIP

If you want to make a bigger shade but don't want to increase the number of cords you use, use a thicker cord.

5 Continue to use a square knot to make eight triangle shapes. Under the second row, make a third row of square knots using two cords from the left knot and two cords from the right knot from the row above (brick pattern). Make three knots, skip four cords and make another three knots. Repeat this all the way around. When you finish you should have four cords between the first set of three knots and the last set you created. There should be eight sets of three knots.

Under each set of three knots, make two knots and then a final row of one knot. This completes the triangle shapes.

If the cords are getting a little unwieldy, group them and tie them loosely together.

6 At the top of a triangle find the outer left cord from a knot on the second row and add a bead.

This cord is the core cord for a clove hitch line (see page 99) running along the edge of the triangle. Each knotting cord is used twice to make a complete clove hitch knot. Use all the cords up to the left anchor cord of the square knot at the bottom of the triangle. Make sure the knots sit tight up against the square knots in a neat line.

7 Repeat step 6 for the other side of the triangle, adding a bead to the core cord. When you reach the bottom of the triangle, use the core cord from the left side as the final knotting cord to close the lines into a tidy triangle shape.

8 Repeat steps 6–7 to make hitch line edges to all the triangles. In between two triangles, pick up the first loose cord on either side (the ones sitting under the beads). Add beads to both cords. These are the anchor cords for a column of square knots. Pick up the next cords down on both sides to create a square knot.

9 Place the cord ends from the square knot just created up over the top of the ring to keep them out of the way. Pick up the next loose cords on each side and add a bead. Make a square knot.

10 Repeat step 9, adding beads to each cord until you have a column of six square knots. Repeat steps 8–9 to make square knot columns between all the triangles.

11 The next stage is to weave the loose cords from the square knot columns over and under all the strands on the sides of the columns.

Pick a column and start with the first loose cord from the top square knot. Take this cord under the first strand, over the second strand, under the third, over the fourth and under the fifth strand. The step photo has the strands numbered to help! Leave the cord hanging and pick up the next loose cord.

12 Alternate the weaving as shown in this step photo. With the next loose cord, you'll start with strand 2 and go under this, then over strand 3, under 4 and over 5.

13 Repeat this with the next three cords from the column, each time you'll have one strand fewer to weave with. The final cord from the fifth square knot will only need to be woven under strand 5. Leave all cords from the bottom square knot alone.

Repeat the weaving on the other side of the column so both sides match. Then repeat for all columns.

14 Working at the point of a triangle, thread a bead on to each loose cord (the ones that you have just woven). Using the two cords hanging down from the bottom of the triangle as the anchor cords, make a square knot with the first cords on either side.

15 Now make four more square knots so you have a column of five. Repeat to make columns under all eight triangles.

16 Weave all the loose cords from the columns so the space between all the columns has evenly woven strands and all the loose cords are at the bottom of the shade facing downward.

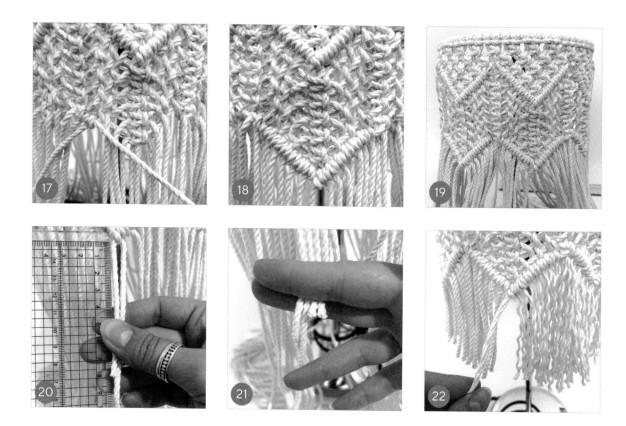

17 This next step is the zig-zag line of clove hitch knots that finishes the design at the bottom (above the fringe). To begin the first hitch line, start at the bottom of a column of six square knots (the ones between the triangles). Find the right-side knotting cord (not the anchor cord!) and use this as the core cord for a line of hitches. Use all the cords up to the left-side anchor cord on the column of five square knots.

18 Move to the six-knot column on your right and find the left knotting cord from the bottom square knot (again, don't use the anchor cords!). Hitch knot to the left using all cords until you meet the hitch line created in step 17. To close the line use the core cord from the left hitch line as the knotting cord for the final knot on this line.

19 Repeat steps 17–18 to make hitch lines all the way around. You'll see that the lines start at the sides of the six-knot columns.

20 The last thing to do is trim all the cords into a neat fringe. Place the shade carrier on the lampstand and put the lampshade on it so you can see the finished height of your macramé lampshade. Decide on the length you want the fringe to be and cut the first cord to that length.

21 Then cut carefully strand by strand around the shade.

22 This type of 3 ply cord looks great as a fringe if you unravel the cords.

cross-body bag

Sian Hamilton

Who doesn't love a bag? Cross-body bags are easy to carry and macramé bags are right on trend. This project is time-consuming but not complex, so if you are a beginner take your time and enjoy the knotting process.

YOU WILL NEED

- Approx 124m (407ft) x 4mm (⁵⁄₃₂in) macramé cord (I used Welcome Yarn by Barbante in Light Grey)
- Working board and clips
- Crochet hook
- 2 x bag handle loops (I used silver 18mm (²³⁄₃₂in))
- 40mm (1½in) toggle-style button
- Super glue
- Masking tape
- Scissors
- Cardboard scraps

1 You need 124m (407ft) of cord to make a bag 22cm (8½in) wide by 26cm (10½in) long. Cut 24 x 4.5m (15ft) lengths of cord, 1 x 1.4m (4½ft) and 1 x 12m (39½ft) piece. This should leave you with a 2.6m (8½ft) piece.

Follow the steps on page 102 to set up a working board. The board needs to have a double line. Use the 2.6m (8½ft) piece as the double line for the working board, fold it in half and clip to the board.

2 Attach all the cords to the double line using lark's head knots (see page 94). Make sure the whole row of knots measures 24cm (9½in).

3 This bag uses mostly square knots (see page 96). To start, make a full row of square knots using all the cords. Work carefully as the cords are very long and can tangle easily. Lay the board down and push all the cords to the right. Separate the cords you are working with, then push them to the left after knotting. This will keep all the cords as tangle-free as possible.

4 Knot three full rows of square knots. On row two skip the first two cords (see steps 8–9 on page 96). This will make the classic brick pattern. The third row will use all the cords, mirroring the first row.

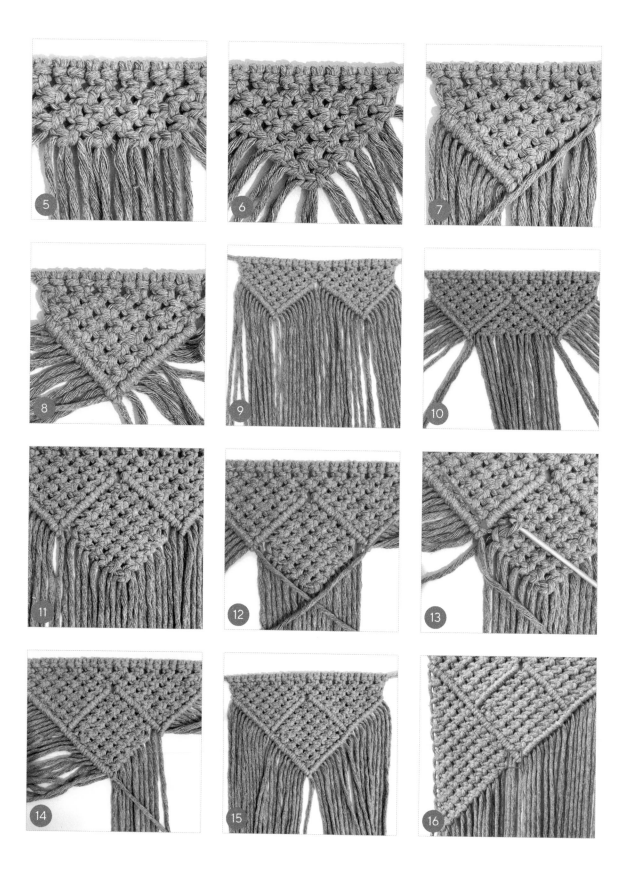

TOP TIP
This bag would look lovely in any colour! Make it simpler by skipping the hitch lines – make a long section of square knots instead and follow the steps to sew up the sides and make a handle.

5 From the fourth row you want to make two large triangles. Skip two cords and make five knots, skip four cords and make five more knots. On the next row (fifth) skip four cords, make four knots, skip eight cords and make another four knots. You should have four cords left at the end.

6 Sixth row: skip six cords, make three knots, skip 12 cords, make three more knots. Seventh row: skip eight cords, make two knots, skip 16 cords, make two more knots. On the eighth row make one knot under the two just made on each triangle.

7 Each triangle is edged with a line of clove hitch knots (see page 99). Pick up the top loose cord on the left side, this is your core cord for the clove hitches. Make a row of hitches using all the cords up to the left side anchor cord on the bottom square knot of the triangle. Find the top cord on the right side of the triangle and use that as the core cord for the line of hitch knots on this side.

8 When you reach the bottom and have used all the cords, pick up the core cord from the left hitch line and use the core cord from the right side as the knotting cord to close the shape.

9 Repeat steps 7–8 on the other triangle but reverse the last knot. Use the core cord on the left hitch line as the knotting cord so the pattern has a mirror finish.

10 Fill in the middle section between the triangles with more square knots. Make five rows of knots, with the fifth row having five knots.

11 The pattern is going to continue in a diamond shape. On the sixth row make four knots, skipping the two left cords from the knot above. On the next row use the two cords from the fifth row (that you skipped in row six) to make another row of five knots. Continue with rows of one knot fewer until you have the full diamond shape, ending in a row of one square knot.

12 The diamond shape is edged with another line of clove hitches. Find the core cords from the hitch lines on the outer edges of the triangles and use these to continue the hitch knots.

13 Place the core cord to one side and find the cord above it by the side of the diamond. This cord should be loose. With a crochet hook pull this cord through the loop on the side of row six.

14 Use the cord you just pulled through the loop as the first knotting cord on the clove hitch line. Continue the hitch knots all the way down to the left anchor cord on the bottom square knot.

15 Repeat steps 12–14 on the opposite side to complete the edge of the diamond. Use the core cord on the right side as the knotting cord, knot it to the left side core cord to close the shape.

16 On the left side come back up the first loose cords and make a square knot. Continue to make rows of knots to fill in the side, making a sideways triangle. When you get to the point of the diamond do not use the last two cords (shown in a red box).

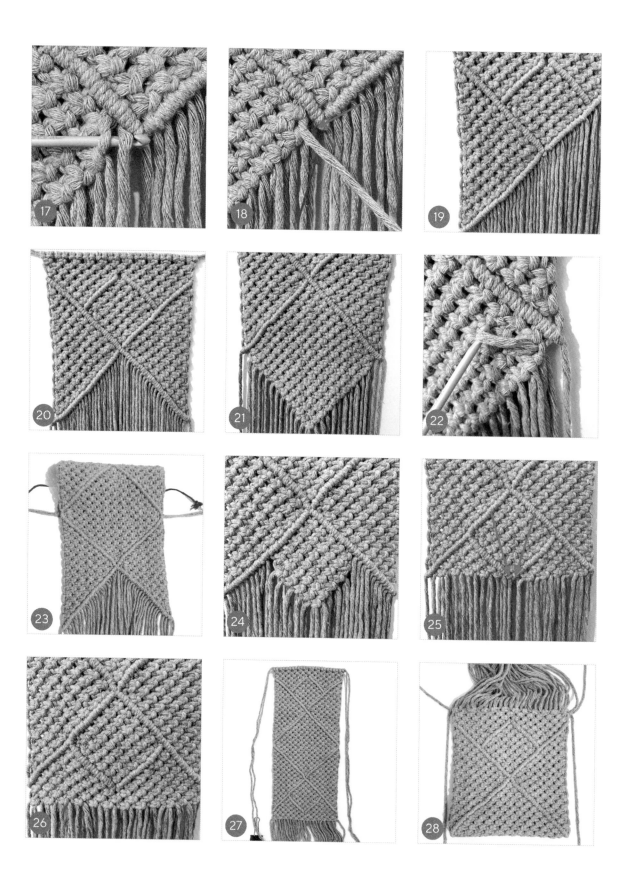

17 Following the same process as you did in step 13, grab the loose cord from the side of the diamond point and pull it through the loop on the left.

18 You should still have another loose cord (shown on the step photo with the red arrow). This is the core cord you now need to continue the hitch line down the side of the square knot shape you have just created. The blue arrow shows the cord you should have pulled through the loop in the previous step – this is your first knotting cord to start the row of clove hitch knots.

19 Knot all the way down to the edge using all the cords.

20 Repeat steps 16–19 for the opposite side to create the same pattern.

21 Fill in the middle with square knots as you did in steps 10–11. Make sure to leave the core cords and one cord next to them loose on either side.

22 On each side find the loose cord that's sitting next to the core cord and, with a crochet hook, pull it through the loop sitting by the side of it. On the left side the loop is on the right and on the right side it's the loop on the left. Pick up the core cord from the hitch knot line and make a line of hitch knots along the edge of this square knot diamond.

23 Repeat the hitch line on the other side of the diamond and then repeat steps 16–20 to create two more sideways triangle shapes with hitch line edges. At this point your macramé piece is quite long, so you might need to pull it up to work on it as it will be hanging off the edge of the board.

24 Repeat steps 10–11 to make a square knot diamond that is 11 rows deep.

25 This diamond has a hitch line edge. Follow steps 12–15, but don't close the shape. Leave the two core cords hanging loose, as shown by the arrows on the step photo.

26 Fill in the two triangles on either side of the diamond with square knots, then add three full rows to mirror the other end.

27 This completes the basic bag. Take the bag off the board, you should have two long cords on either side at the top.

28 Fold the bag in half, matching the edges.

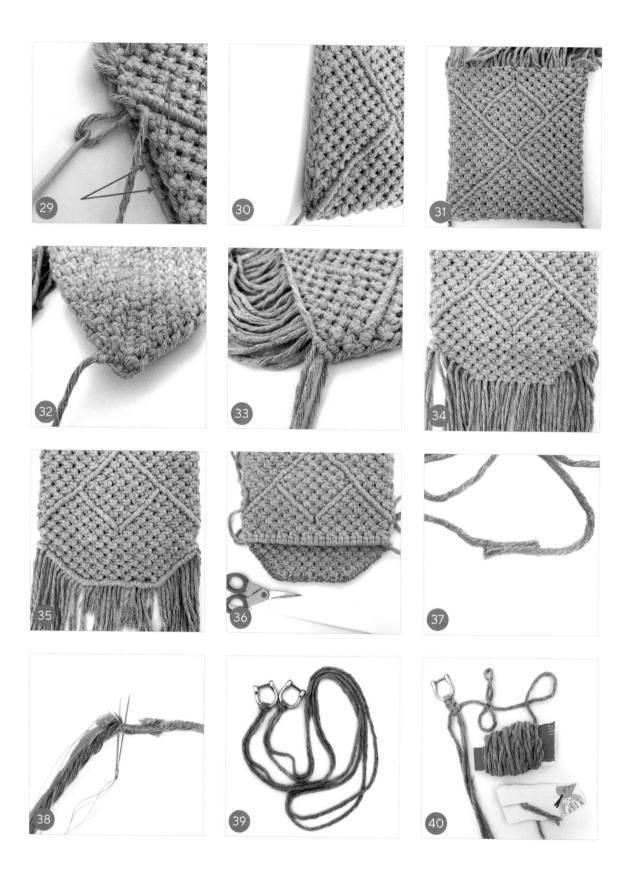

29 The next step is to sew up the sides to make the bag shape. Use one of the long cords from the top edge (the ones that were clipped to the board).

You will see on the sides that there are loops between the square knots. On the step photo, red arrows show the front loops and blue arrows show the back loops. These are used to sew the sides together. Using a crochet hook to help pull the cord through the loops, sew down, pulling the cord through a loop on the front then one on the back and doing what should look like a diagonal running stitch.

30 When you reach the end, gently pull the cord tight.

31 Repeat for the other side of the bag.

32 You will have the two cord ends on the bottom corners after you have stitched up the sides. These need to be poked through to the inside of the bag with the crochet hook.

When the cords are on the inside, pull the bag inside out. This is tricky as the macramé is stiff, but persevere. When the bag is inside out, use the crochet hook to loop the cord ends through a couple of close loops and knot the cord to secure it.

It doesn't matter what loops you use as you just want to secure the ends so they don't come undone when you use the bag. Cut off any excess cord.

33 Turn the bag right side out. On the open edge, find the second long cord that was clipped to the board. You should have one on either end (by the sewn-up sides). Make three clove hitch knots on each side, using the closest loose cords.

This bag design has a flap and toggle button as a closer but you could make an open-topped bag if you wish. If making an open-topped bag, continue to hitch knot all the loose cords. When you get to the end and have knotted in all the cords you can either leave the ends as a fringe or add a little glue and cut them off. Before you cut all the cords off, leave two of the longest cords on each side to attach the handle and go straight to step 37 to make the handle.

34 To make the flap, knot six rows of square knots, reducing each line by one knot to bring the sides in at an angle. Refer to the step photo for guidance.

35 On the left side find the core cord with the three hitch knots from step 33. Use this core cord to continue the hitch line all the way around the square knot flap.

36 To finish the bag, put a tiny amount of glue on the inside edge of the hitch line around the flap. This is to ensure that it doesn't come apart when the bag is used. Cut off all the excess cord ends.

37 To make the handle, pick up the 1.4m (4½ft) piece of cord you cut in step 1. Find the ends and place them side by side facing each other. You are making a big loop!

38 Using a needle and thread, sew these ends together. Wrap the thread as tightly as you can around the ends and then sew through the whole lot until it feels solid. Pull on the cord to make sure it will not come apart.

39 Add the handle loops to the cord with lark's head knots.

40 Find the centre point of the 12m (39½ft) length of cord and mark it. Get two scraps of cardboard and wrap the cord around them, starting at both ends and wrapping until you have a workable section free in the middle with the ends wrapped around the card. It's impossible to keep this length of cord tangle-free unless you use card.

41 The handle is a row of square knots. Pick up one end of the handle with a loop attached and place the marked centre of the 12m (39½ft) cord behind the handle cords (they are now the two anchor cords). The 12m (39½ft) length is your knotting cord. With the centre behind the anchor cord, start making square knots.

42 I hung my handle loop on a hook on a door as it made it easier to do the square knots, with gravity helping hold the anchor cords steady. Knot all the way to the other handle loop and cut off any excess cord. That completes the handle.

43 To attach the handle to the bag, find the longest two cords on each side and wrap them twice around the straight bar on the handle loops, leaving a 2.5cm (1in) gap between the bar and the bag.

44 Bring the ends of the cord back down toward the bag and use them to make square knots on the section between the handle and bag. Cut off any excess.

45 Add the toggle button in the centre of the flap with the needle and thread. Grab a scrap of cord and make a loop for the toggle. Make a large knot in the end of the loop and push the loop through the bag from the inside at a point where it is in line with the toggle.

There were a lot of scraps of cord with this project so I used some to make tassel features. To make these, double up pieces of cord, push them through the edge of the flap and make lark's head knots. Add as many as you wish and cut them level so they look neat. This finishes the bag off nicely.

star and moon wall hanging

Tansy Wilson

Metallic macramé twine suits this project perfectly, as do these wire frames. The project focuses on the star, but the steps are exactly the same for the moon or indeed any shape of your choice.

YOU WILL NEED
- 3mm (⅛in) metallic macramé twine
- 22cm (8½in) star and 20cm (8in) moon metal shaped frames
- Scissors
- 10mm (⅜in) bead with 4mm (⁵⁄₃₂in) hole for each design

1 Cut 6 x 3.5m (11½ft) lengths from your silver 3mm (⅛in) macramé twine and fold each piece in half. Tie on to the bottom of your star using the lark's head knot (see page 94), so that three pairs are on the left point of the star and three pairs on the right. Starting with the left point, take the far right-hand cord of the six and pull diagonally left across the front of the other cords. This will be your lead cord.

2 Tie the remaining five cords hanging to the left along this lead cord using clove hitch knots (see page 99).

3 Go back to cord 6 and pull this far right-hand cord diagonally left across the front of the other five cords. This will now be your lead cord.

4 Tie the remaining five cords hanging to the left along this lead cord using clove hitch knots.

5 Move to the right point and repeat the process of tying a matching pair of clove hitch knots along two lead cords, this time from left to right.

6 Make a square knot (see page 96) using the four central cords: two from the left section and two from the right section – cords 5, 6, 7 and 8.

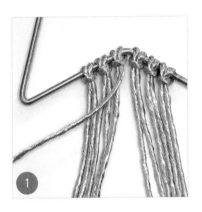

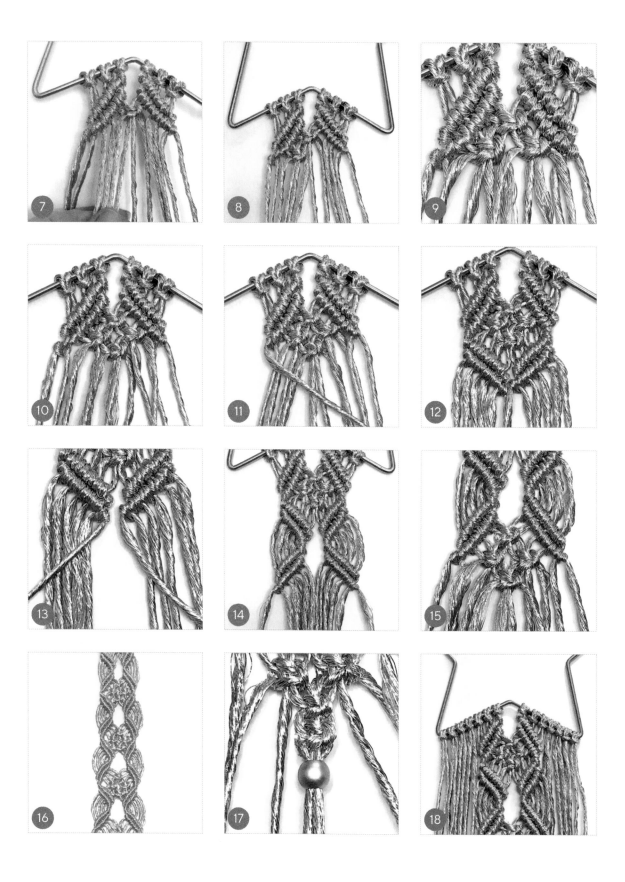

7 Take the two left-hand cords coming out of the bottom of the square knot and the next two cords immediately to the left of these.

8 Make a square knot using the cords selected in step 7.

9 Take the two right-hand cords coming out of the bottom of the square knot made in step 6 and the next two cords immediately to the right of these, and tie another square knot so it is in line to the right with the one created in step 8.

10 Make another square knot with the central four cords – cords 5, 6, 7 and 8.

11 Take the far left-hand cord from the left section and pull it to the right diagonally across the front of its five partner cords. This will now be your lead cord.

12 Tie clove hitch knots with the remaining five cords from this section along this lead cord.

Then take the far left-hand cord again and repeat to produce two rows of clove hitch knots. Move to the right section and repeat the process, tying a matching pair of clove hitch knots along two lead cords, this time from right to left.

13 Take cords 6 and 7 and pull diagonally in front of their partner cords, as in this image, to create two new lead cords.

14 Tie clove hitch knots along these lead cords as you have done before in steps 4–5 so you end up with two rows either side on each section.

15 Tie four square knots in the same formation as before in steps 7–10.

16 Keep repeating the pattern so you build up a long wavy vertical line of knots.

17 When you reach your desired length, create a tassel by tying three square knots on top of each other with the four most central cords and pushing a large-hole bead up to meet them.

18 Now cut 8 x 1m (3ft) lengths of silver macramé twine, fold each one in half and attach four to the left point and four to the right point. Depending on the size of your wire frame you may need to cut more or fewer.

TOP TIP

The metallic twine is very slippery and unravels easily, so be prepared for a slightly looser macramé pattern.

19 You can leave the design here and trim the bottom of your hanging into a lovely shape. The metallic twine unravels very easily, so a fluffy fringe is easy to achieve.

Edging Detail

20 I decided to cover my frame using continuous lark's head knots. For this you will need around six times the length of the wire plus twice the length of the fringe. This star needed 5m (16½ft). Attach this length to the wire frame using a lark's head knot, but do not fold it in half to do this. Instead, measure the length from the star to the bottom of your fringing. This is the point where you fold the twine and create the knot. This leaves you with one piece that blends into the fringe and another length of more than 4m (13ft).

21 Take the length and, working always to the right of the lark's head knot, take the twine in front of the wire frame, around the frame and then over the twine itself, as in this image, then pull.

22 For the next knot take the twine behind the wire frame, around the frame and then through the twine and pull down. Keep alternating one in front and one behind until you reach the other end, where you can trim your remaining twine to the same length as your fringe.

mini totes

Sian Hamilton

Liven up a tote bag with a unique macramé edge. This project uses mini tote bags that are perfect as a lunch pack, but these designs would also be great for larger, shopper-style totes.

YOU WILL NEED

Red tote
- 4mm (⁵⁄₃₂in) macramé cord (I used Welcome Yarn by Barbante in Red)

Grey tote
- 4mm (⁵⁄₃₂in) macramé cord (I used Welcome Yarn by Barbante in Dark Grey)
- Mini jute tote bags
- Needle and colour-coordinating thread
- Board and clips
- Scissors
- Bristle brush

RED TOTE

1 Follow the steps on page 102 to set up a working board with a red cord line.

2 Cut 24 x 1.2m (4ft) lengths of cord. Fold in half and attach to the line with lark's head knots (see page 94). When all the cords are attached, lay the bag down and make sure the width of the attached knots is the same as the width of the bag.

3 Make a row of square knots (see page 96). Make sure the width still matches the bag.

4 Split the knots into three groups of four knots. Place the middle set of knots out of the way and make a triangle of square knots on both sides. To do this you need to skip the two left cords from the first knot on the top row and use the two right cords with the two left cords from the second knot on the top row (see steps 8–9 on page 96). Make three knots on the second row, two knots on the third row and one knot on the fourth row.

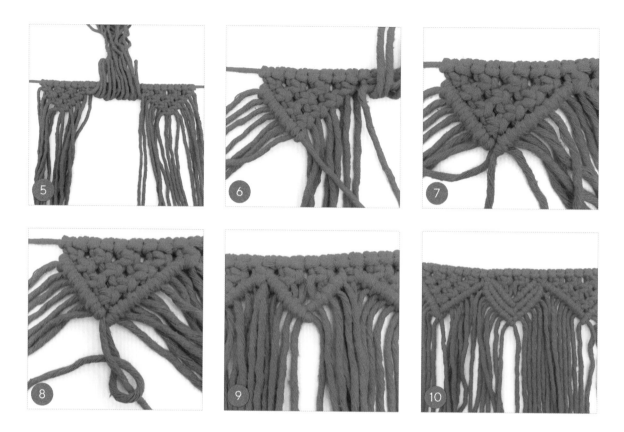

5 Repeat to make an identical triangle on the other side.

6 This design has a clove hitch line running down the sides. Pick up the outer cord on the left side. Use that as the core cord for the clove hitch line, use the second cord in as the first knotting cord. Make a line of hitches (see page 99), using all the cords up to the left side anchor cord on the bottom of the square knot triangle.

7 For the opposite side of the triangle, use the left cord from the fifth knot on the top row as the core cord. Hitch knot down to the bottom of the triangle. Stop when you get to the other hitch line.

8 Pick up the core cord from the left side hitch line and use the right-side core cord as the knotting cord to close the point of the triangle.

9 Repeat steps 7–8 to make a hitch line around the right side triangle. In the middle of the design, on the top row find the two centre square knots. From the knots either side pick up the outer cords and use them as the core cords to make a diagonal hitch line around the two centre knots. When you have used all the cords, use the right side core cord as the last knotting cord to close the shape.

10 You should have loose anchor cords from the square knots sitting either side of the centre knots. Use these as the core cords to make two more lines around the centre triangle. The point of this triangle shape should now be level with the triangle points on each side.

TOP TIP
If creating a design for a larger shopper bag, use the steps on page 93 to work out how long the cords need to be.

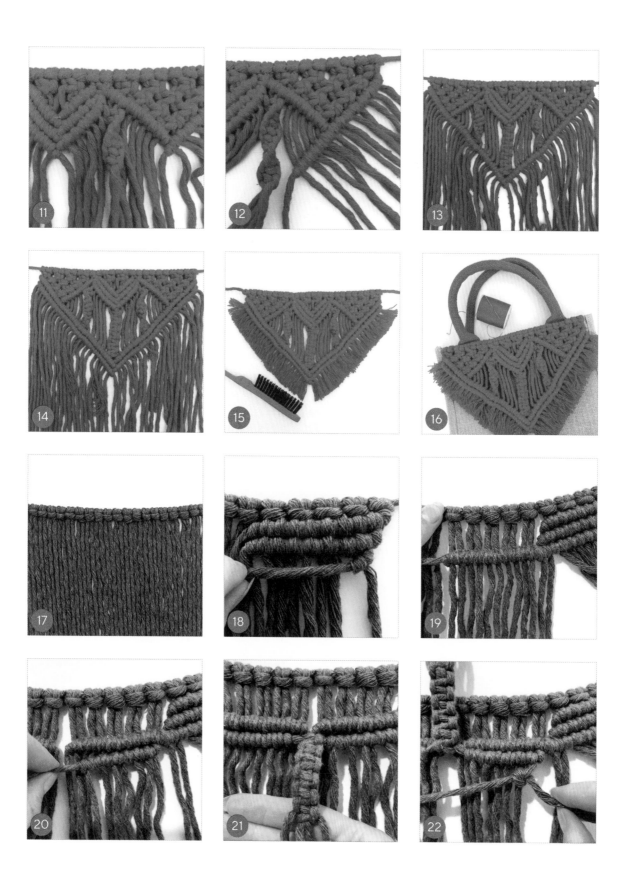

11 Between the triangles, pick up one cord from the centre triangle and three cords from the side triangle and make a column of 11 half square knots (see page 98) with a twist going left on the right-side column and a twist going right on the left-side column. The twists should be facing inward.

12 Find the core cord from the hitch line on the outer edges of the design and continue the line, making clove hitches with all the loose cords on the outer side of the columns.

13 Find the centre four cords under the middle triangle (with three hitch lines) and make a column of 12 square knots.

When that column is in place, continue the hitch lines from step 12. Continue on a 45-degree diagonal line so the design is one large triangle. As you get to the point of this large triangle, use the core cord from the right side as the last knotting cord to close the shape.

14 Add a second hitch line under the line just completed.

15 Take the design off the working board. Trim all the cord ends to your desired length. Then brush the cord out with a bristle brush. Cut down the side cords from the top edge, but leave about 5cm (2in) each side.

16 Sew the design to the tote bag, tucking the cords on the sides in. I used colour-coordinated thread to match the macramé and sewed through the lark's head knots at the top and the top edge of the bag.

GREY TOTE

17 Follow steps 1–2 to make up a working board, cut 20 x 1.4m (4½ft) lengths of grey cord and attach with lark's head knots to the line on the working board.

18 Start on the edge (left or right) and pick up the outer cord. This is going to be the core cord for a clove hitch line. Make hitch knots with nine cords – this should use the cords from five lark's head knots. Make two more hitch lines underneath. Repeat on the other side.

19 On both sides, continuing to use the core cords from the third row of hitch lines, use up all the loose cords until the two lines meet in the middle.

20 From the left edge, count nine cords across and use the 10th cord as the core cord for a second hitch line. Knot using seven cords. After repeating this line on the right side this should leave six cords loose in the centre.

21 In the middle, find the two core cords from the top lines and the two core cords from the second lines. Use these to make a column of six square knots.

22 Now make a third hitch line using the outer cord from the second line as your core cord. Knot with four cords.

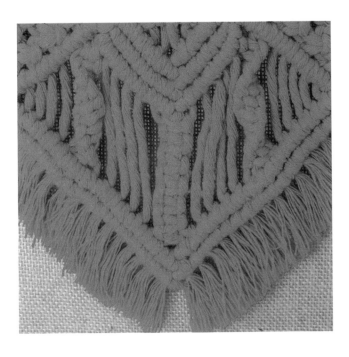

23 Repeat on the other side. Check your hitch lines mirror each other on either side of the centre.

24 Add another row of hitch lines. Skip the two loose outer cords and use the third as the core cord to make a hitch line using all loose cords until it meets in the centre.

25 This should use six cords on each side as knotting cords.

26 The next hitch lines are made using the fourth cord from the centre as the core cords.

27 Knot using six cords towards the outer edges. Repeat on the other side.

28 The next set of hitch lines is a little tricky to start. The core cords are the outer cords from the square knot column and the first knotting cord is the core cord from the hitch lines made in step 24. They will be behind the column. Use the core cord from the right-side line as the first knotting cord on the left-side hitch line (as shown in the step photo).

29 Repeat for the other side. Use the left-side outer cord on the column as the core cord and find the core cord from behind the column for the first knot.

30 Knot using eight cords on each side. Keep the hitch lines tight up against the lines above.

31 The next set of lines are three rows around the base of the column. From the column on the left side, skip a cord and use the second cord out as the core cord. Moving right, use the cord by the side of the column as the first knotting cord.

32 Knot across to the right, using four cords including the anchor cords on the column. Pick up the second loose cord on the right side (shown with a red arrow) and use that as the core cord for a hitch line back the opposite way towards the left. The first knotting cord on this second row is the cord sitting to the left of the core (shown with a blue arrow).

33 Knot across using eight cords, then reverse the way the core cord is facing and use the last cord knotted as the first knotting cord on another line going towards the right.

34 Knot a line using nine cords, the eight from the line above and one from the right side to anchor the line in place.

35 To make the tassels, gather all the cords below the central section you have just completed. Push the other loose cords out of the way. Grab one of the central cords and make a large loop with the end of the cord facing upwards (as shown in the step photo). Find the core cord from the bottom hitch line and place it behind the gathered cords. Keep it separate, going off to the side.

36 Pick up the core cord that's sitting off to the left side and wrap it around all the gathered cords while holding them tightly with your free hand. Wrap four times.

37 Hold the wrapped section with your free hand and find the loop you created in step 35. Thread the end of the wrapping cord through this loop. See page 100 for more instructions on how to make an edge tassel.

38 Continue to hold the wrapped section and pull on the end of the cord that's facing upwards out of the wrapped section. The loop under the wrapping should move and pull the wrapping cord inside the wrapped section. You will need to pull hard. Do not pull it all the way up, just far enough that you cannot see the end of the wrapping cord. Trim off the end you have been pulling level with the wrapping.

39 Repeat steps 35–38 to make tassels under all the sections on the design. Take the macramé off the working board and trim the side lines to approx 5cm (2in).

40 Pick up the bag and clip the macramé to the top edge. This will hold it in place as you sew. Tuck the side ends under the design close to the top edge so they get sewn in too.

41 Sew along the edge, making sure you sew through the macramé and the bag.

42 When the sewing is complete, trim the tassels to your desired length. I choose to make them mirror the triangular shape of the design.

43 To finish, brush out the tassels with a bristle hair brush and trim the ends again to tidy them up.

jam jar to glam jar

Tansy Wilson

An old jam jar can be dramatically transformed with this project. I have given measurements for the jars I have used, but yours may be different sizes. The simple rule is to always count cords in fours. So if I've used 16 cords and your jar is slightly bigger, the next number of cords to use will be 20, then 24, and so on. The design combinations are endless, so you can get really magical with your macramé.

YOU WILL NEED
- 2mm (1⁄16in) household string
- Scissors
- Selection of jam jars

LARGE JAR
1 This jar is 20cm (8in) high and 40cm (16in) diameter.

Using 2mm (1⁄16in) parcel or household string, cut 2 x 60cm (24in) lengths and set one piece aside. Tie the other 60cm (24in) length loosely around the neck of the jar, using a bow so you can undo it if necessary. I'll call this cord the top cord for the following steps.

2 Cut 48 x 1m (3ft) lengths of the string. Taking one at a time, fold each piece in half and tie on to the top cord using a lark's head knot (see page 94).

3 When you have added all 48 pieces, if you need to you can undo the bow and re-tie to tighten the top cord and make all 96 x 50cm (20in) lengths of string hanging down sit nice and close to each other. Select the first four lengths of string that sit directly underneath the knot of the bow.

4 Tie three square knots (see page 96) directly under each other on these four strings.

5 Take the next four strings along and again tie three square knots directly under each other on these four strings. Repeat this step so you have chunky vertical rows of square knots going all the way around the jar.

6 Pick up the remaining 60cm (24in) length cut in step 1 and hold it horizontally, directly under the last row of square knots. I'll call this cord, the horizontal lead for the following steps.

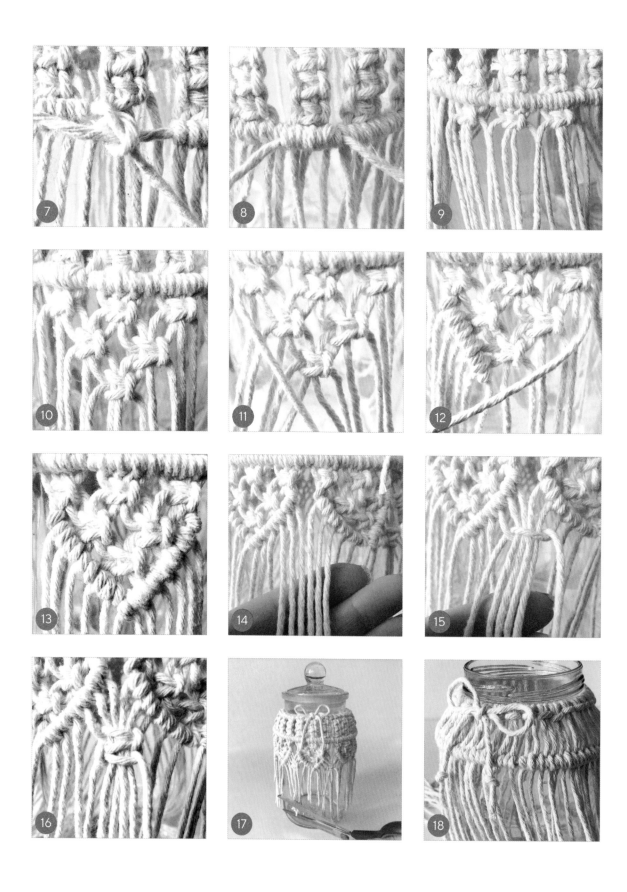

Starting at any point towards the back of the jar, pick up a string and tie a clove hitch knot (see page 99) around this horizontal lead. Take the next string along and repeat. Try to keep this horizontal lead as close to the underside of the square knots as possible and work methodically around the jar.

7 Before you get to the last four strings coming out of the remaining square knot, cross both ends of the horizontal lead across each other so there are now two horizontal leads to tie the last four clove hitch knots on to.

8 Next, simply pull each end of the horizontal lead in opposite directions and it will pull all the clove hitch knots tightly together and secure the horizontal lead very firmly to the macramé. Trim the excess lengths of horizontal lead away using sharp scissors.

9 View the jar from the front bow and select the four strings that hang directly below the horizontal row completed in step 8, that were also used in step 4 to create the first vertical line of three square knots directly below the knot of the bow. Tie a square knot. Take the four strings to the left of this square knot and tie another square knot. Now take the four strings to the right of the central square knot and tie another square knot to the right, so you end up with three square knots in a row.

10 Tie two square knots underneath the row of three created in step 9 by missing out the first and last two lengths of string. Then tie a final knot at the very bottom to form a triangle pattern.

11 Take the left-hand string hanging down from the bottom of the top left-hand square knot in the row of three created in step 9 and use this as your lead string.

12 Make clove hitch knots around this lead string with each adjacent string hanging down until you get to the bottom square knot, where you will only use the two left-hand strings hanging from the bottom of this knot.

13 Take the lead string coming out of the bottom of the top right-hand knot in the row of three created in step 9 and use this as your lead string. Tie clove hitch knots along it to meet the two final right-hand strings coming out of the bottom of the single square knot created in the middle at step 10. Finally you can join these two lead cords together by choosing one to be the lead string and tying another clove hitch knot.

14 Repeat steps 9–13 so you make eight triangular patterns going around the jar. I then took three strings coming out of the right-hand side of one triangle and three strings coming out of the left-hand side of the triangle immediately next to it. A total of six strings.

15 Start to tie a square knot with the first and sixth strings, keeping it loose so you don't bunch up the middle four strings.

16 Complete the square knot, then tie a half square knot (see page 98) to create one-and-a-half square knots or a zig-zag knot.

17 Repeat steps 14–16 to tie zig-zag knots between each triangular section. You can then use scissors to trim all the strings either in a straight line or to echo the points of each triangle.

MEDIUM JAR

18 This jar is 17cm (6¾in) high and 32cm (12¾in) diameter.

Cut 3 x 50cm (20in) lengths for horizontal pieces and set two aside. Tie one piece loosely around the neck of the jar as the top string, then cut 32 x 1m (3ft) lengths of string. Fold each one in half and add to the top string using a lark's head knot. Tighten the top string by tightening the bow if necessary. Then, as in steps 6–8, add another 50cm (20in) horizontal length, securing it in place using clove hitch knots just where the shape of the jar changes.

19 Make a row of square knots all around the jar under this second horizontal string.

20 Now add your final 50cm (20in) horizontal length of string, securing it exactly as in steps 6–8 with clove hitch knots.

21 Directly under this final horizontal string, create another row of square knots all around the jar. Then create another row of square knots below, missing the first two strings so that the second row of knots staggers. I finished off the design by featuring triangles and tying two square knots on top of each other, missing every fourth string. Trim the ends with scissors.

SMALL JAR
22 This jar is 12cm (4¾in) high and 25cm (10in) diameter.

For a much simpler design you can create a more open macramé pattern. Cut 1 x 40cm (16in) length and tie a bow loosely around the neck of the jar for the top string.

Cut 16 x 60cm (24in) lengths, fold them in half and tie on to the top string using the lark's head knot.

Space these 32 lengths evenly around the top string, as they won't fit snugly together, and tie eight square knots.

23 Take the bottom two right strings from one square knot and the bottom two left strings from the next knot along and tie another square knot. Keep the distances all the same to create an even open pattern. Repeat around the jar.

24 Tie a final row of square knots under this second row, again taking the bottom two right strings from one square knot and the bottom two left strings from the next knot along and keeping the distances all the same. Trim the ends with scissors.

TOP TIP
Using 2mm (1/16in) parcel string is a cheap alternative to actual macramé cord. You can also use garden twine for a rustic look. There really are so many combinations to play with.

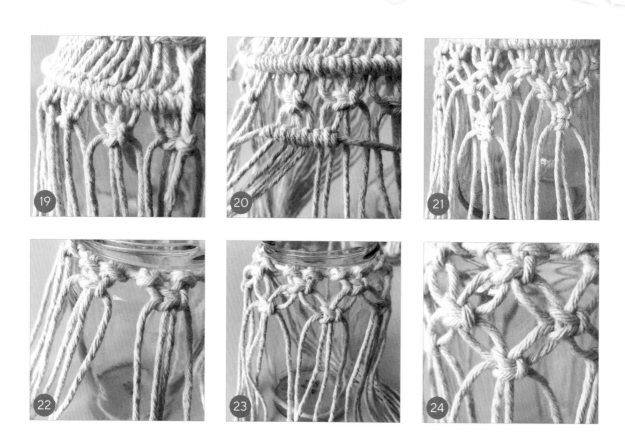

tasselled cushions

Sian Hamilton

Macramé cushions are all the rage right now! Make your own tasselled cushion fronts to liven up any chair.

YOU WILL NEED

Pink cushion
- 3.5mm (approx ⅛– ⁵⁄₃₂in) macramé cord (I used single twist cotton cord in Antique Rose)

Purple cushion
- 3mm (⅛in) macramé cord (I used 3 ply cord in Blackberry)
- Needle and colour-coordinating thread
- 40cm (16in) cushion cover
- Board and clips
- Scissors
- Bristle hairbrush

PINK CUSHION

1 Follow the steps on page 102 to set up a working board. For a 40cm (16in) cushion cut 36 x 1.3m (4ft 3in) lengths of cord. If your cushion is larger you will need more cords. Fold in half and secure to the line on the working board with lark's head knots (see page 94).

2 This pattern is made up of clove hitches (see page 99) and square knots (see page 96). Each section of clove hitches uses six cords. To start the clove hitch, pick up the outer cord on the left side. This is your core cord to knot on to, and you need to hold it at an approx 45-degree angle to the rest of the cords. Pick up the cord next to it and create a clove hitch knot. The core cord should always be in front of all the other cords. The knotting cord comes up from below the core cord and wraps around it to create the knots. You knot each knotting cord twice to create a clove hitch.

3 Make a line of clove hitch knots using five cords. Count across six cords and use the sixth as your next core cord. Hold this one at a 45-degree angle facing left. Knot clove hitches that match the angle of the line you've just completed. You are aiming to create a downward-facing triangle shape.

4 Make a second line of clove hitches underneath the two lines you already have. Use the outer cords on each side as your core cords.

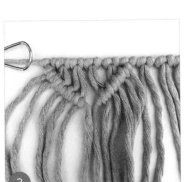

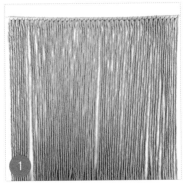

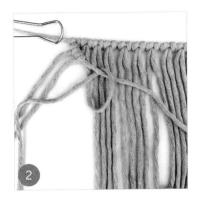

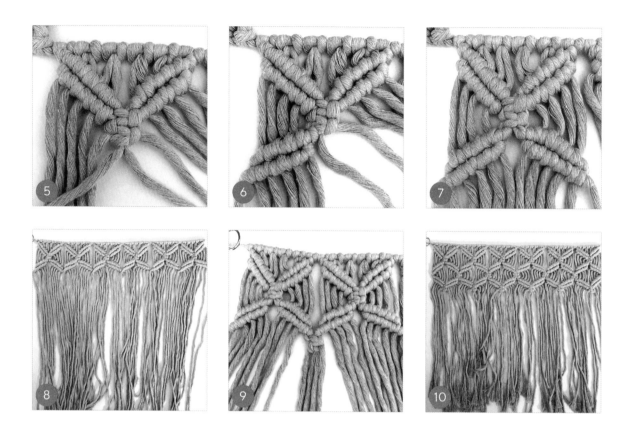

To link these angled lines together, this pattern uses square knots. Make a square knot using the core cords from the first lines as the anchor cords. Make the knot with the two core cords from the second lines.

5 Make a second square knot using the same cords.

6 Pick up the left-side anchor cord from the square knot and use that as the core cord to make a new line of clove hitches at a 45-degree angle to the left. Use all the cords on this side and make a second line underneath.

7 Repeat step 6 to make two lines on the opposite side.

8 Repeat steps 2–7 to make a set of six cross shapes using all the cords. Try to keep them as level with each other as possible.

9 The crosses are all separate, to anchor them together make sets of two square knots between each cross. This should mirror the square knots at the centre of the crosses.

10 Make another row of clove hitch lines using all the cords. Repeat the design using double lines of hitches and double square knots between the lines to make the a row that should look like diamond shapes. This pattern continues to repeat to create the whole design.

TOP TIP

This design would make a lovely full downward facing triangle. Increase the length of the cords (2–2.2m (6½–7ft 3in) on a 40cm (16in) cushion) to make them long enough to do this.

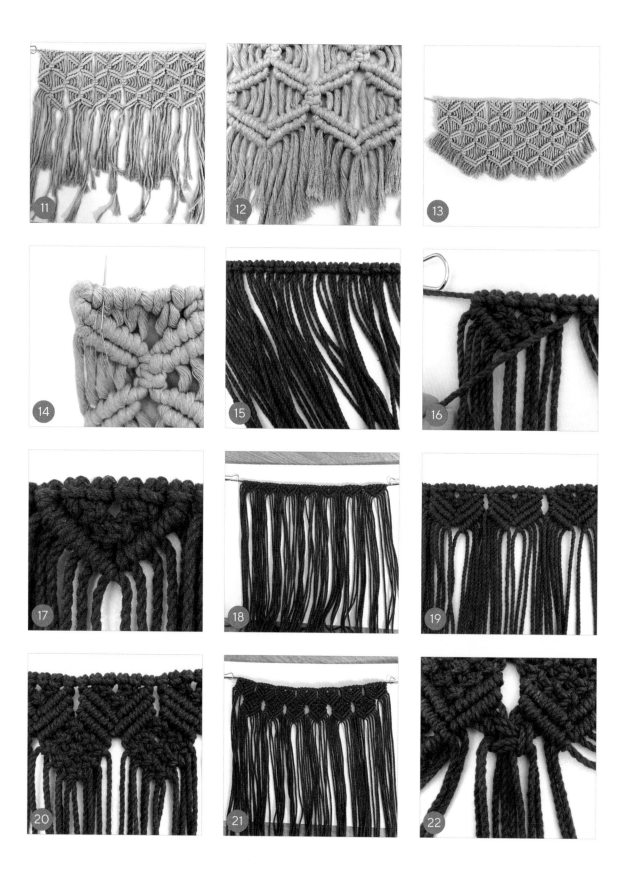

11 Repeat step 10 but leave out the outer set of cords on each side. Start this row using the right-side anchor cord from the square knot above as the core cord. You should have six cords loose on either side of the design.

12 Repeat step 11, leaving 12 cords loose on either side. This is the final row. When you have created all the lines, they will be open at the bottom. To link the clove hitch lines together to close the diamond shapes you need to do one extra clove hitch using the core cord from the right-side lines as the knotting cord.

Pick up the core cord from the left side and use the core cord from the right side as the knotting cord to close the lines and make pointed downward facing triangles. Repeat for the second line of hitches.

13 When you have finished the final row, you need to trim the fringe so it is level. Take the macramé off the working board and use sharp scissors to trim the cord ends. I trimmed up to the shortest cord. You will find that all the cord ends are different lengths even though they all started at the same length. If you want a fluffy edge, brush the cord with a nylon bristle styling hairbrush. Cut off the excess line that was holding the macramé to the board, leaving about 4cm (1½in) each side so the outer lark's head knots don't fall off.

14 Attach the macramé design to the cushion cover with a sewing needle and thread. You can pin the design to the cushion front, but I found it easy to just hold it in place and sew through all layers. Make sure to tuck the line cord on each end under the design so it gets sewn in to secure it. This design is only attached at the top, loose at the sides. You can sew down the sides as well if preferred.

PURPLE CUSHION

15 Follow step 1 to set up the working board and cut 36 x 2m (6½ft) lengths of cord. Attach to the board with lark's head knots.

16 Starting on the left, skip the first two cords and then create two square knots. Make a third square knot centrally below the first two. On the left side pick up the outer cord and use that as the core cord for a line of clove hitch knots running along the edge of the square knots. Stop the line when you have used the left side anchor cord from the bottom square knot. Repeat on the other side.

17 When you reach the bottom, pick up the core cord from the left line and use the core cord from the right line as the last knotting cord to close the triangle shape.

18 Repeat steps 16–17 until you have seven triangle shapes using all the cords.

19 Add two more lines of clove hitches to each triangle. Close the second line as you did in step 17. Don't close the third line, leave both core cords hanging down.

20 Starting on the left, use all the cords in between the first and second triangle to make a diamond shape of square knots. This should be rows of: one knot, two knots, three knots, two knots and one knot. Repeat along, making six diamonds in total. You should have unused cords at either side.

21 Under the square knot diamonds, add two lines of hitches using the outer cords as the core cords. Repeat for each diamond and make sure both lines are closed (as in step 17).

22 The next row across will be large square knots between the diamond shapes. Start with the first and second diamond. Pick up the four top cords (two from the left and two from the right) – these are the anchor cords for the square knot. Pick up the next two cords on either side to create the square knot. You should have two cords loose on either side. Repeat between all the diamonds. You should end up with five large square knots in total.

23 Under each large square knot, create a line of clove hitches continuing to use the core cords from the lines above. Close the lines as in step 17.

24 Repeat step 20 to create another row of four diamonds and step 23 to create hitch lines under the diamonds.

OPTIONAL TASSELS
25 I decided to make long flowing feature tassels on this design. You can either do the same or continue the design into a full triangle. Follow the steps on page 100 to tie a tassel.

26 Tie all the tassels but don't cut off the ends yet. Take the design off the board and cut off the excess line, leaving about 4cm (1½in) on each side.

27 Sew the design to the cushion as in step 14.

28 This 3 ply cord doesn't comb out as nicely as the single twist cord does, but it's got a nice wavy finish if you unravel each one into the separate three cords. When you've unraveled them all, trim the ends so that they sit level with each other and skim the cushion edge. If you don't want the tassels to drape over the cushion edge, trim them to the length you desire.

tools, materials and tips

CORDS

Macramé can be done with pretty much any type of cord: embroidery thread, hemp, rattail, cotton, paracord and more. The one rule to keep in mind is that the thicker the cord, the chunkier the design will be when finished.

BOARDS

For small projects you can get macramé boards, which are thick foam boards that you can push pins into to secure work. These boards have a slotted edge to hold excess cords in place as you work. They are good for miniature designs or jewellery. If working larger projects, you may need a hanging pole rather than a flat board.

PINS

T-pins are thick pins with a T-shaped top that are used for pinning cords to boards if working flat, to hold them in place. They are available from lots of suppliers who also sell macramé supplies.

You can also use standard dressmaking pins, which are finer so a little harder to handle. The ball-ended ones are good, as the ball helps you to grip the pin and place it in the board.

T-pins are sturdier, so if you are using a specialist macramé board, it would be a good idea to invest in these.

SCISSORS

You will need a pair of sharp scissors to cut the cords and trim edges. It's a good idea to keep scissors for this sort of craft separate from ones you use for paper, etc, as paper can dull the blade and make the scissors hard to use for things like cord and threads.

Dressmaking scissors are very sharp because they are made for cutting through fabric, so they work well on cord or twine. The size of the scissors you need will be determined by the design. The larger the design, the larger the scissors. Don't try to cut a neat fringe end on a large design with nail scissors, as it just won't work!

GLUE

If you want to glue the ends of your designs, you need to use a glue that will dry clear. An all-purpose craft glue works well, though takes time to dry, so remember to leave it to dry completely. For paracord or any other artificial fibre cords, you can use super glue. Super glue dries immediately but can leave a darker area where the glue is, so use it carefully and sparingly.

TOP TIPS

- If you are using a cord that frays too much, use a small piece of tape on the ends of each cord to hold the threads together.

- Glue ends to secure them if you are making bags that will get a lot of use. Only glue if you can hide the ends, as glue often darkens the colour of the cord. Do a test piece before adding any glue to a project.

- Use a comb to brush out the ends of strands into a fringe.

- Watch out for artificial cord materials like paracord getting twisted. This type of cord can naturally twist itself around. You want to try to keep your cords straight, as it will affect the final look of the design if you weave them with an unwanted twist in the cord.

- Be mindful of using cords like hemp and metallic ones for items that will sit against skin. These types of cord can be scratchy and result in pieces that are not comfortable to wear.

- Watch the tension! Some cords or threads can have a little stretch in them, so don't pull them too tight. Keeping the knots tight is key, but overtightening will change the design and result in work that will not lay flat and will look uneven.

- Mock up designs on paper first. It sounds a little strange but if you are working on a new freehand design, it's a good idea to sketch it out so you have something to follow.

- When cutting lengths for a new design, be generous with the length, as designs heavy in knots can reduce in finished length by 75 per cent. Always cut lengths that are at least three times the finished length you desire, unless it's a very open design.

cord calculations

All the projects in this publication give you the amount of cord you need if using the same thickness that the project suggests. If you want to use a different thickness of cord then you'll need to work out how much cord you require for the project.

1 Tape a pen or thin pole (I used a crochet hook) to your work surface and attach a length of cord in the thickness you are going to use. Fold the cord in half and use a lark's head knot (see page 94) to attach it to the pole – these are your anchor cords. Cut a separate piece of cord to use to make a square knot. Place this behind the anchor cords. Tie one complete square knot (see page 96).

2 Pull the knot tight and measure the depth of the knot. In this example the knot is precisely 1cm (²⁵⁄₆₄in) deep.

3 With a marker pen, draw lines at the edges of the knot, shown with blue arrows.

4 Undo the knot and lay the cord out so you can measure the distance between the two marked lines. This example measured just under 10cm (4in).

You now need to do a little calculating!

CALCULATIONS

If you know the number of square knot rows – for example, if the finished project has 30 rows of square knots, you need to multiply that by the length of each knot – 10cm (4in) – which is the measurement you discovered in step 4.

Example

Number of rows (30) x length of each knot (10cm/4in) = 300cm (120in), so that means you need each working cord to be 3m (10ft) long.

If the project has a finished height but not a fixed number of knot rows, you need to do a different calculation.

Divide the finished height of the project by the depth of a single knot – for example, for a project that's 25cm (10in) high, the calculation is:

Example

Finished length (25cm/10in) divided by knot depth (1cm/²⁵⁄₆₄in) = 25 knots.

Multiply the number of knots (25) by the length measured in step 4, the amount of cord you need for each knot.

Number of knots (25) x length of each knot (10cm/4in) = 250cm or 2.5m (100in or 8ft 3in per working cord).

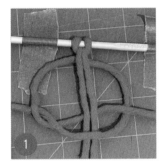

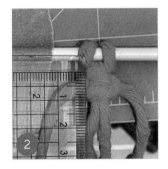

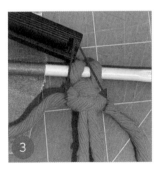

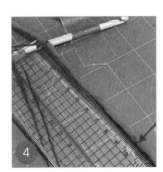

lark's head knot

This knot is the one used to secure all the cords to the base pole, large jumpring, pole or other item that you are weaving on to. For this technique we'll simply call it a bar. The lark's head knot is a very useful knot to know for jewellery making – you can attach a cord necklace to a pendant using this knot.

1 When starting any project, the first thing to do is cut all the cords you need. Always be generous if you can so you have extra length to play with. To start the lark's head knot, fold the cord in half with the ends meeting and place the looped (folded) end behind the bar.

2 Bring the two cord ends over in front of the bar and thread them through the loop.

3 Pull the cord ends to tighten the knot to the bar. You need to make sure your knots are tight before you start working on the piece. Repeat this knot to attach all the cords you need for your project.

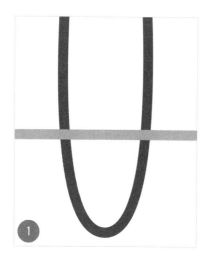

square knot

This knot is the one that you probably recognise as the macramé knot, as it's the most widely used.

1 Attach all the cords you need to the pole with lark's head knots (see page 94). These illustrations show the set-up for one square knot.

2 To illustrate this knot clearly, the outer left cord is coloured pink and the outer right cord blue. The two cords in grey are called the anchor cords – they will stay in place as you use the two outer cords to make the knot. Bring the left-side outer (pink) cord across in front of the two anchor (grey) cords and under the right outer (blue) cord.

3 Pick up the right outer (blue) cord and bring it behind the two anchor cords and through the loop created in the left outer (pink) cord.

4 Pull the two outer cords tight – this creates the first part of the square knot. **Note:** this is a half square knot. If you want a twisted spiral design, keep repeating this half of the knot – as you go, you'll see the knots naturally spiral in a twisted column (see page 98).

5 You now want to repeat the first part of the knot going the opposite way to create a full square knot. Bring the right outer (pink) cord across in front of the two anchor (grey) cords and behind the left outer (blue) cord.

6 Bring the left outer (blue) cord behind the two anchor cords (grey) and through the loop created in the right outer (pink) cord.

7 Pull the outer cords tight to finish the square knot.

8 This knot creates a brick-style pattern as you add rows. On the second row, skip the first two cords and use the right-side anchor cord and the right-side outer cord (blue) from the left knot above. Use the left-side outer cord (pink) and the left-side anchor cord from the right knot above. The two anchor cords (shown in grey) are now the cords used to make the knot.

9 Follow these steps to continue adding square knots. Pull the knots tight up against the row above.

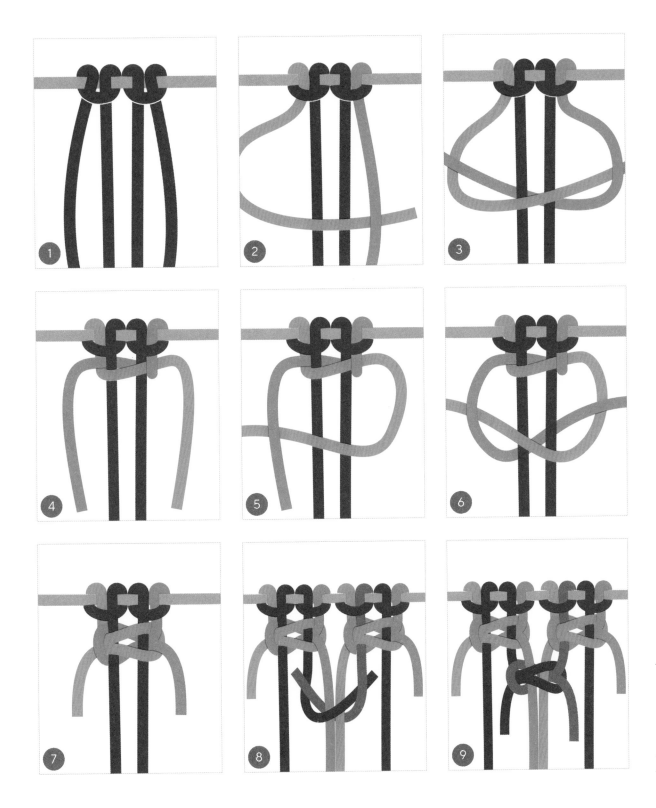

half square knot

This uses the same technique as the standard square knot but repeats half of the knot over to make a column of knots that twists.

1 This knot requires four cords, two centre cords as anchor cords (shown in grey) and two knotting cords (shown in pink and blue). Bring the left-side knotting cord (pink) cord across the two anchor cords and behind the right-side knotting cord (blue).

2 Bring the right-side knotting cord (blue) up and behind the anchor cords, making sure it is under the pink cord. Pull it through the loop made with the pink cord on the left side.

3 Pull this knot tight. This is a half square knot.

4 Repeat steps 1–2 to make more square knots. Make sure each time you bring the left-side knotting cord in front of the anchor cords and the right-side knotting cord behind the anchors.

5 You will see the column of knots twist as you repeat the knot. The column will twist to the right side. If you want a column to twist to the left, reverse the knotting cords in step 2, so bring the left-side knotting cord (blue) in front of the anchor cords and under the pink cord. Bring the pink cord behind the anchor cord and through the blue loop. This will result in a twist going towards the left.

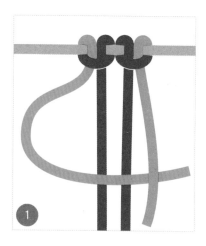

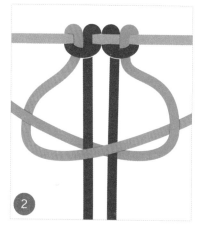

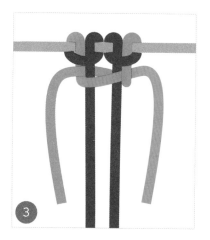

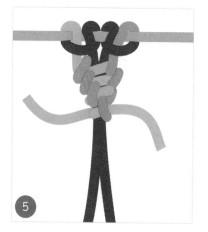

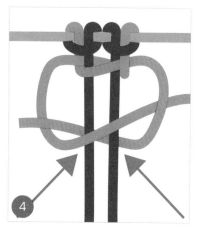

clove hitch knot

This knot is also known as double hitch knot, forward knot (in friendship bracelet-making) and double half-hitch knot. This knot makes a nice tight row of knots and can be done straight across the piece or in a diagonal, leaving space above.

1 Start with a row of cords attached to a pole with lark's head knots (see page 94), or if finishing off a piece then start on the left side of the section you are working on. Take the outer left cord, shown in pink, and bring it across all the other cords. This pink cord is the one you are going to knot on to. It's called the core cord. In some projects it's called a static line.

2 Holding the core (pink) cord towards the right, pick up the next cord shown in blue – this is the knotting cord. Bring the knotting (blue) cord behind the core (pink) cord out towards the left, then bring it over the core (pink) cord and back

under the core (pink) cord and through the loop created in the knotting (blue) cord.

3 Pull the knotting (blue) cord tight and repeat step 2 to create an identical knot. This knot is mostly used as a double.

4 Pick up the next free cord shown in green – this is now the knotting cord. Repeat steps 2–3 to make the next clove hitch knot.

5 Pull the knot tight and repeat as many times as needed. This knot can take practice to make it nicely uniform, as it's easy to overtighten the knot or not tighten it enough. So keep an eye on how it's looking and make sure you are being consistent with how tight you make the knots. Use your thumbnail to push the knots up next to the previous one to keep a tight line.

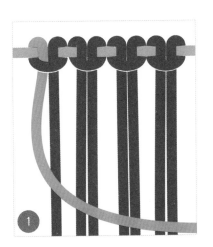
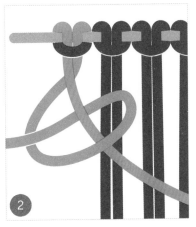

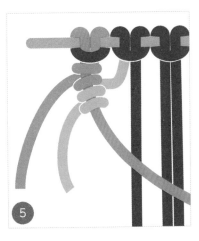

edge tassel

Finishing the edge of your macramé design with an edge tassel is a great way to complete a design.

1 Gather the cords you want to make into a tassel and grab another cord on the macramé or cut a separate piece of cord to use as the wrapping cord. In this technique the wrapping cord is shown in pale pink, so it is easy to see. Place the wrapping cord behind the tassel cords. One end should be sitting in front of the tassel cords and have a loop on the bottom end with the end of the cord facing upwards. The other end should be at a right angle and should be the longest end, as this is the end that will wrap around the tassel.

2 Pick up the wrapping cord and wrap a column around the tassel cords. Start at the top end and wrap down four or five times. Take the end of the wrapping cord through the loop.

3 Pull on the end of the wrapping cord that is sticking out of the top of the wrapped column until the loop and bottom end of the cord disappear inside the column.

4 Trim off the ends level with the column.

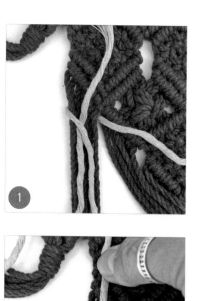

scrap cord tassel

The best way to use up long lengths of scrap cord is to make tassels!

1 Lay the scrap cords down gathered together – use as many or as few as you wish. Make sure on one end the scraps are level, and this will be the bottom of the tassel. The other end (top end) is likely to have lots of different lengths: these will be trimmed off at the end. Find a long scrap cord and make a loop with it on the top end (shown with the red arrow).

2 Pick up another long scrap of cord, lay it down behind the gathered cords so that one end is at a right angle (shown with the blue arrow – this end is the wrapping cord) to the gathered cord, and the other end is in front, with the end facing upwards (shown with a red arrow).

3 Pick up all the cords, holding them with your free hand on the top end. Make sure you are holding the wrapping cord with the same hand. Tightly wrap the wrapping cord around five or six times to create a wrapped column.

4 Thread the wrapping cord through the loop that should be sitting below the wrapped column. Check out step 2 of the edge tassel technique opposite, as this clearly shows the same step.

5 Find the end of the loop cord. You might need to pull gently on the loop to find the correct cord at the top end of the wrapped section. When you have the correct cord, pull the loop end up underneath the wrapped section. Pull until the wrapping cord disappears up inside the column. Don't pull too far – you want the cord to be trapped inside the column, not pulled through to the top. See step 3 of the edge tassel technique opposite.

6 Trim all the ends away at the top end, leaving the one cord that made the loop in step 1 in place.

7 Use a bristle hairbrush to brush out the cords to make a lovely fluffy tassel. Trim the ends after brushing for a neat finish.

working board

If working on a small piece of macramé that does not have a firm pole, branch or ring to wrap the lark's head knots around, you might find a working board useful.

The board can be any type of thick board: 5mm (³⁄₁₆in) foam board from craft shops is perfect, or a piece of thin plywood works well too. Clips are available from many stationery supply stores and craft shops. The foldback type work well here.

To set up the board, cut a piece of the cord you will be using for the project and clip it tightly to the board with the foldback clips. This gives you a working line to attach your macramé cords to. If the line stretches as you work, open the clips and pull it tight again.

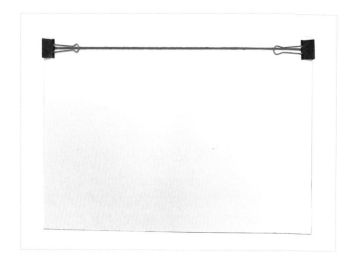

simple hanging line

When you create a macramé piece you'll need to hang it nicely. This is an easy technique for making a simple hanging cord.

1 Cut a generous length of twine to suit the size of panel you are making. Make a loop on one end with one side approximately 15cm (6in) in length, the other end should be very long. Fold the loop in half over itself. Slide a pole or piece of driftwood through the loop so it goes over the two outer pieces of twine, but under the two central pieces, as in this image.

2 Pull the twine tightly, and in effect you have created a lark's head knot at the very end of a length of twine. Repeat at the other end of the twine. Pull the twine tightly and you will have made a neat and tidy way to hang any panel. You can adjust the central hanging piece by loosening one end and pulling the cord. Cut the twine off at the back of the pole or knot each end and trim to make a feature tassel.